WHY MARRIAGE COUNSELING FAILS

IS THE PROBLEM THE MARRIAGE— OR THE COUNSELOR?

DR. DAVID HAWKINS

Licensed Clinical Psychologist with 40+ Years of Experience

WHITAKER HOUSE

All Scripture quotations are taken from the *Holy Bible, New International Version*®, NIV®, © 1973, 1978, 1984, 2011 by Biblica, Inc.® Used by permission of Zondervan. All rights reserved worldwide. www.zondervan.com. The "NIV" and "New International Version" are trademarks registered in the United States Patent and Trademark Office by Biblica, Inc.®

WHY MARRIAGE COUNSELING FAILS
Is the Problem the Marriage—or the Counselor?

MarriageRecoveryCenter.com
www.youtube.com/user/drdavidbhawkins
www.instagram.com/marriagerecoverycenter
www.facebook.com/marriagerecoverycenter

ISBN: 978-1-64123-848-9
eBook ISBN: 978-1-64123-849-6

Printed in the United States of America
© 2022 by Dr. David Hawkins

Whitaker House
1030 Hunt Valley Circle
New Kensington, PA 15068
www.whitakerhouse.com

Library of Congress Cataloging-in-Publication Data (Pending)

1 2 3 4 5 6 7 8 9 10 11 **LLJ** 29 28 27 26 25 24 23 22

CONTENTS

PRELUDE:
STACY AND KEVIN

Stacy sat on the edge of her bed, clutching her leather-bound journal, pen in hand, ready for any incredible insights. She thought back to how she had fallen head over heels for Kevin. He was the talkative one in their youth group at church; she was quiet and insecure. She hoped he would notice her, but he always seemed to be pursuing her friends.

She had fantasized about Kevin for months before he crossed the room to talk to her. She held her breath as he came into the room, greeting everyone as he entered. He stopped in front of her and asked if the seat next to her was available. She nodded, he smiled, and she got lost in his bright blue eyes.

After the group meeting was over, he walked out with her as they left the church. Time passed and they became friends, then close friends, and finally sweethearts.

After dating for two years, they married. What a lovely wedding they had! Stacy still remembered the butterflies in her stomach and the tears in his eyes as she walked down the aisle to join him. They shared dream after dream of what their marriage might be. Children, yes. Travel, of course. A house of their own that she would decorate, absolutely.

That was three children ago. That was before he became immersed in his work as the chief diesel mechanic at a local trucking company. It seemed the more responsibility he took on at work, the less time he had for her.

Every morning, Stacy had thirty minutes to herself before getting the boys up and ready for school and herself ready for work. She wanted this time to be nourishing. She wanted clarity, to find a sense of direction for her frustration. She'd read that she needed to take time for herself, but lately, rather than a time of thoughtfulness and peace, her morning solitude left her feeling even more restless. Every day, she felt a cloud of darkness crash in on her as she faced the realities of her unhappiness with her marriage.

Kevin wasn't a bad man. He was solid, practical, and hardworking. His moods were stable...boringly stable. Still, Stacy felt alone and unhappy and couldn't understand why. She no longer shared her heart with him, and he no longer asked about her heart the way he had when they were younger. All he talked about was work, and he asked only perfunctory questions about the boys' schooling. Ten years of marriage, three children, and his long hours on the job all seemed to sap Kevin and Stacy's enthusiasm for each other.

Was he as unhappy as she? If they were *playing house*, she was not having fun. What was wrong with her? Did all married women feel this way?

From all outward appearances, Stacy and Kevin were successful. They had a lovely house on the edge of town. They had friends from church. They were close with Kevin's brother and his wife, as well as Stacy's sister and her husband.

She heard the boys waking and tried to get her thoughts to take some clear form, but it was all a muddled mess in her head.

Once again, she remembered the tears in Kevin's eyes as she walked down the aisle at their wedding. Were those days totally gone? Could they be brought back?

She put her journal down, pulling herself back to the present. She wouldn't think about her marriage. She had other things to do.

THE WORK OF
LOVE AND MARRIAGE

Love does not obey our expectations; it obeys our intentions.
—Lloyd Strom

Every marriage begins with lovely words, words of commitment, undying love, and the promise of years of bliss together. These are meaningful, poignant moments. Any of us who have crossed the threshold from singleness to married life have uttered some words of commitment, and we meant them. Certainly, the vows we take at the start of a marriage, filled with hope, are spoken from a very emotional and heartfelt place.

However, there is little or nothing mentioned at the altar about the day-to-day issues involved in marriage. Not many wedding ceremonies warn of the challenges of two becoming one.

Our wedding vows, our spoken words of commitment, contain no mention of the hardships every couple is likely to face. Typically, things don't work out the way we believed they would before we said them. How could they? We can't see into the future. We don't really know what we're getting into when we commit to a lifelong attachment to another human being.

Now, don't get me wrong. While I offer a sober, precautionary tone at the very start of this book, I champion marriage. I am happily married. My point is that our initial vows and our best intentions fall apart at some point because they are simplistic, often failing to take all of the pertinent issues into consideration.

While we plan to be selfless, to give selflessly to our mate for the entirety of our marriage, these intentions give way to the reality of our limitations. We believe we will be giving, kind, and caring; perhaps we even imagine we can be this way forever. But this is incredibly naive and shortsighted! With every good intention to be selfless and magnanimous, we can easily slip into being selfish and immature, small and petty, causing severe problems in our marriage.

The sobering truth is this: marriage requires work and selflessness at times. This is challenging for even the most mature person. We mean well, but in a moment of agitation, threat, or fear, we react immaturely.

Imagine two immature people in the throes of conflict, agitated and reactive, having long forgotten their vows to be giving and loving. Imagine these individuals, caught up in a difficult moment, with no intention of being selfless. In a moment, shortsighted naivete gives way to reality.

To be fair, most of us are neither selfless nor selfish but somewhere in the middle. We are capable of being naive and very hopeful, filled with good intentions, but in a moment, we are also capable of dropping our guard and ruining a situation.

We don't plan on being destructive. We don't plan on being hurtful. But feeling hurt ourselves, we become self-protective and respond by hurting others. There are many skills we didn't learn from our parents or haven't developed during our adulthood. Even a hint of this selfishness can cause significant damage.

These are the moments when marriage really takes work. We must summon our maturity, which can be incredibly challenging. If our skills for dealing with adversity have not been previously developed, these difficult moments will turn into difficult days, perhaps even weeks. Tragically, we can end up with difficult, contentious lives.

Again, our shortsighted naivete about what we hope and wish our marriage will be crashes into harsh reality. Truthfully, most of us don't rise to the level of a challenge but rather fall to the level of our limited skills. This is a painful truth. Can you see the problem? Armed only with good intentions, and shortsightedness about how we are going to face impending challenges, we slip into destructive behavior patterns. One negative interaction, layered upon a previous wound, leads to an even greater marital slide.

Where this marriage trouble begins is where the work of love and marriage becomes even more critical. It requires us to let go of simplistic views of marriage and embrace the difficult truths, the bigger challenges.

THE PROBLEM OF NAIVETE

The adventure of marriage begins with at least some simplistic hopefulness. Who would set out on such an adventure with doom and gloom in mind? It's very natural and understandable to enter into matrimony with happy expectations.

Naivete—a lack of experience, wisdom, and judgment—is part of our nature. It takes significant time, intention, and experience to let go of such innocence. This is especially true when it pertains to how we function in marriage. We cannot predict all of the pitfalls in a union of two separate people, with two separate histories and the inherent baggage that comes with that.

We cannot be mature, ready to be selfless and giving while also being unaware of the challenges inherent in a marriage. Filled with hope, wonder, excitement, and a strong dose of naivete, we enter the challenges of marriage largely unprepared, untrained, and unskilled. Is it any wonder then that we fairly quickly end up in marital trouble?

My experience as a marriage counselor has taught me that most couples have no idea about the real work involved in love and marriage. They have no idea how to face the challenges of love and marriage. They make feeble attempts, cobbling together snippets of skills they read about in some book, or meaningful words they heard at a marriage retreat. While there is much to be learned from all of the books and retreats, it simply isn't enough. Marriage takes continual work.

MOST COUPLES HAVE NO IDEA ABOUT THE REAL WORK INVOLVED IN LOVE AND MARRIAGE.

It is no surprise that many, if not most, couples are unaware of the dangers and challenges in marriage. Uninformed and unprepared, they face some of the most significant relational challenges possible. Perhaps it is the most difficult work any of us will ever face. Getting marriage right is tough work.

UNPREPARED FOR THE CHALLENGE

Remember Stacy and Kevin? Were they prepared for the challenges of marriage, or were the challenges hidden by the stars in their eyes? They were in love and had talked about a magical future together, but these were dreams, not reality. Had they learned anything prior to marriage that would help them in their relationship? Not likely.

Honestly, most of us don't really know what we're doing when it comes to relationships. It's a bit like being a passenger on an airplane and being told in the midst of turbulence that you need to bring the plane safely down for a landing—when you have no experience as a pilot. Heart racing, palms perspiring, thoughts a scrambled mess, you're told it's up to you to save the day.

Most of us enter marriage with hearts coming out of our heads but without any hands-on experience. We simply begin marriage ill-equipped for the challenges of a life together.

Malcolm Gladwell, in his book *Outliers: The Story of Success*, is famous for saying it takes 10,000 hours of practice to become an expert.[1] Gladwell cited examples of accomplished musicians in Berlin practicing 10,000 hours, the Beatles practicing 10,000 hours in the early 1960s, and Bill Gates putting in 10,000 hours of programming work before founding Microsoft.

The accuracy of this 10,000-hour rule is not the point I'm making, but what Gladwell pointed out is proficiency at *anything* takes a lot of practice. Each week, my piano teacher tells me, "It's not practice that makes perfect, but perfect practice that makes perfect." Trust me, there is a big difference between the two.

And so, we enter marriage inexperienced and unprepared, thinking, "It can't be that tough. I love my spouse, and along with my marriage vows of commitment, we'll grow together."

Wrong! I often use Gladwell's' 10,000-hour rule to ask couples how much time and effort they've put into perfecting their marriage. Here's what they've told me:

+ We've read some books.

+ We've attended a couple of marriage retreats.

+ We've gone to marriage counseling a couple different times.

Oh, my! We continue to believe love and good intentions will sustain us. We believe we will figure it out with practice. We believe it *can't* be that difficult. Right?

BUT MARRIAGE *IS* DIFFICULT

Look, marriage isn't actually *just* difficult. It's nearly impossible. There are many challenges every couple faces as they enter into marriage.

Again, consider what is taking place. Two people from different worlds, often with different and differing values, with their unique set of self-defeating behavior patterns, are coming together as one. This is, at best, a challenging endeavor.

---

1. Malcolm Gladwell, *Outliers: The Story of Success* (New York: Little, Brown and Company, 2008).

Let's look at some *huge* issues that couples commonly face:

1. *Communication Issues.* You have two different people, from different locales, different family backgrounds, and different cultures, perhaps one an introvert and the other an extrovert, trying to communicate effectively. Remember, most have no training, skills, or experience with communicating effectively, except for what we observed with our parents, which may very well have been bad training.

2. *Boundary Issues.* The art and science of cultivating, establishing, and maintaining boundaries is the stuff of many best-selling books. Couples often don't know or understand what is their business and what is not, when to say something to their mate and when to be quiet.

3. *Sexual Issues.* Many couples have sexual intimacy issues. With unresolved emotional issues, sexual intimacy is nearly impossible. Emotional and relational issues create an impossible, tension-filled atmosphere, making sexual intimacy hard to achieve.

4. *Financial Issues.* Many couples struggle to make their money last longer than the month. One might be a spender and the other a saver. Learning how to talk about, explore, and resolve these issues is often a very difficult endeavor.

5. *Differences in Values.* Many couples believe they will naturally be compatible, but this is often challenging because we are all different. One might be more conservative spiritually, politically, or financially than the other. Unless they have learned how to show grace to the other, conflict arises.

6. *Poor Conflict Resolution Skills.* This can become overwhelming if the couple has not learned basic conflict resolution skills. Fighting, squabbling, bickering, and horrific power struggles are often the result.

7. *Emotional Abuse Issues.* This is a huge issue that's often hidden; it's defined by patterns of abuse of power and control, selfishness and emotional immaturity. Often hard to see, nearly impossible to define and understand, emotional abuse left unchecked and untreated will ruin a marriage.

These are just a few of the *huge* issues facing most marriages. They don't often stand alone, but are often layered, one on top of the other. Can you see the magnitude of the problem? With so many pitfalls and barriers to intimacy and connection, is it any wonder why so many couples are in significant marital trouble?

Add to these daunting challenges the fact that most couples spend very little time considering the issues harming their relationship or how to resolve them. Here again is the issue of shortsighted immaturity and naivete about how to resolve complicated issues. Denial, effective in the short run, allows a couple to make one day more tolerable than the one before, but as time progresses, that avoidance of conflict is devastating.

Denial creates an overwhelming dilemma. Issues mount and hard feelings accumulate, creating distance and causing even more conflict. How do couples entering into marriage learn of these dangers? How do they let go of their naivete and face reality, ready to move forward prepared?

MOVING FROM "ME" TO "WE"

It has been rightly said that the only way to effectively deal with problems is by facing them. This is especially true in a marriage. One of the more concerning issues many couples avoid is the importance of moving from "me" to "we."

Think about it. While growing up, we have been encouraged to become individuals. We have been taught to embrace our individuality—to champion it, in fact. We have been taught to celebrate our uniqueness.

Then, in a moment, we're expected to set aside at least part of our individuality so that we can embrace our connection to this other person, our mate. This can be confusing and overwhelming; many don't face this challenge well.

Recently, I happened upon an intriguing article entitled "The Number One Reason Marriages Fail" by Dr. Neil J. Lavender.[2] Dr. Lavender debunks the notion that marriages fail because of all the reasons I just

---

2. Dr. Neil J. Lavender, "The Number One Reason Marriages Fail. It's a reason that no one ever talks about," *Psychology Today*, June 22, 2017 (www.psychologytoday.com/us/blog/the-two-shall-become-one/201706/the-number-one-reason-marriages-fail).

cited. While he agrees they are certainly valid issues that certainly contribute to marriage problems, Lavender maintains they are not *the central issue*.

The central issue, he says, is that most couples fail to truly become a couple. He writes, "Two separate and uniquely different people come together to form a whole whose essence is greater than the sum of its parts, and not two individuals who are constantly 'hijacking the we' by trying to make their partner become more like them."[3]

Dr. Lavender's position holds some truth and points to another aspect of the enormous challenge of marriage: selfishness. Let's consider selfishness again. After over forty years of counseling, I see spouses trying to make their partners do things their way, think their thoughts, and follow their lead. At the worst, this is appropriately called coercion and manipulation.

Why would we expect anything different? Remember, marriage is two different people, with differing views and values, attempting to come together as one. This is a tall order. Uniting two very different people is a bit like tying the tails of two cats together. The extrovert often tries to get the introvert to *do more things*. The introvert often tries to get the extrovert to *slow down*. The saver tries to get the spender to tighten the budget, while the spender tries to get the saver to loosen up. Both try to manipulate the other, coercing one another to change, which more often than not results in resentment.

Making matters even worse, each person assigns the other the responsibility of making them happy, another sign of failing to move from *me* to *we*. "I'd be happy if he/she would [*fill in the blank*]." Many people truly believe this. They believe and rehearse the notion, "I'd be happy if only they would…"

As you might imagine, this mindset results in misery and resentment. This is a plan destined to fail. No other person should hold the power to make us happy. No one person should hold the power to make us miserable. These expectations and the ensuing power struggles create massive resentment and animosity, with each partner becoming even further entrenched in their position. Positions taken, sides drawn—the war is on. Couples end up angry, hurt, and contemptuous of their mate, leading to further erosion of a marriage.

3. Ibid.

OUR BEST THINKING

In spite of this, we must bear in mind that couples entering marriage are doing the best they can. They haven't been taught about all the issues I've previously cited. They haven't learned about the importance of moving from me to we. They are entering this new relationship with limited understanding and equally limited skills.

NO ONE SHOULD FEEL LIKE THEY FAILED OR BE BLAMED FOR BEING IN MARITAL TROUBLE.

The hard work of love and marriage is…well, real work. Our best thinking is not likely to get us very far. No one should feel like they failed or be blamed for being in marital trouble. *The vast majority of married couples are in trouble in some way. The problem is epidemic.* The obstacles are significant, and our preparation for marriage and creating a cooperative relationship is limited. While we may have been taught that marriage isn't that difficult, this simply isn't true.

The twelve-step process of Alcoholics Anonymous has a wonderful saying that's worth sharing: "Your best thinking got you here. Right here, where you are today."

Pause and let those words sink in. We have limited skills and our best thinking will take us only so far. Believing that our best thinking will surely carry us forward is shortsighted.

Our best thinking is so very limited. Remember, the work of love and marriage is real work. Our best thinking, without intervention and expert assistance, often keeps us stuck and moving in exactly the same direction—or backward.

Our best thinking created a series of building blocks leading us to a point of difficulty. Remember, we didn't arrive where we are by some spontaneous action. Rather, we arrive where we are by a long series of steps, actions we've taken, and habits we've learned. We have created exactly the life we have. We've arrived at where we are because of years of practicing bad behavior, poor communication, challenged problem-solving, and ineffective conflict resolution skills.

I know these are hard realities, but too many marriages suffer because of this kind of flawed thinking. We must start with reality so we can change the way we're getting help—or not getting help—to build much healthier relationships.

HIDDEN HABITS

Let's return to Stacy and Kevin's story to see if we can discover the origins of their problems. Learning to be self-reflective, self-critical, and insightful are all prerequisites for having the kind of joyful marriage you want.

Stacy and Kevin are in trouble. Let's consider a few of the hidden barriers and limitations impacting their marriage:

1. *Both exhibit magical thinking.* They both naively believed their relationship would function well due to their commitment to one another. Neither anticipated or prepared for the challenges of marriage—of two different people becoming one.

2. *Kevin appears to be married to his work.* He is so focused on his work, he has little time or energy for creating a loving, dynamic relationship with his wife. Marriage takes focused time and attention, and Kevin may be working too much to give his marriage the care it needs.

3. *Stacy feels alone and lonely.* She longs to have a lively, communicative relationship with Kevin. She perceives him as being disinterested in a deeper connection. This issue needs to be addressed in a critical conversation.

4. *Stacy has growing depression that requires attention.* With a tendency to avoid issues, Stacy is slipping into a depression, withdrawing

more and more from Kevin. She needs to develop assertiveness skills, along with healthy boundaries.

5. *Neither one shares their heart with the other.* The chasm between Kevin and Stacy is growing, and they are in danger of creating an even deeper disconnection from one another.

6. *Both live in denial of the problems.* Neither Kevin nor Stacy has the courage or the knowledge to confront the other on the direction of their marriage. Neither has the courage to talk about the loneliness in their marriage. If these problems are allowed to continue, only more trouble will occur.

When I hear the story from Stacy's point of view, I am deeply concerned. While her issues are not unusual, they are likely hidden from her. This is often the way problems develop, one issue at a time, building on the last. Said another way, dysfunctional patterns of relating are likely denied and thus unavailable to them for insight, growth, and change.

FOUR HORSEMAN OF THE APOCALYPSE

While Stacy and Kevin's problems haven't yet reached a crisis point, it will come to that if they are not addressed. Marriages are fragile and need tender loving care to survive.

Dr. John Gottman, author of the well-respected book *Why Marriages Succeed or Fail*, has identified four patterns of interaction that predict whether a marriage will succeed or fail.[4] His research confirms what I have seen in my practice. There are predictable patterns we know can lead to serious marriage issues and possible divorce.

Gottman's four patterns are worth all of us knowing, understanding, and applying to our marriage.

1. *Criticism.* Gottman makes it clear that criticizing your partner is not the same as offering a critique or voicing a complaint. Making a specific complaint, about a specific issue, is very different from attacking your mate's character. Imagine the following:

---

4. John Gottman, *Why Marriages Succeed or Fail: And How You Can Make Yours Last* (New York: Simon & Schuster, 1995).

    A. *"You will never change."*

    B. *"You spend too much money."*

    C. *"You can't be honest."*

2. *Contempt.* Gottman discovered couples in trouble communicate in disrespectful ways. They may use mockery and sarcasm as a way to make a point. They mimic their mate, roll their eyes, or simply walk away when their mate is talking. Imagine adding the following to the exchange:

    A. *"Where did you learn that, from your mother?"*

    B. *"Really?"*

    C. *"I'm just doing the same thing you always do."*

3. *Defensiveness.* Many of us experience occasional defensiveness, but when it is a pervasive pattern and reaction to any concern brought to us, change cannot occur, growth is stifled, and issues cannot be resolved. Defensiveness typically escalates a conflict because it often involves shifting the blame, playing the victim, or simply avoiding taking responsibility for bad behavior. Imagine the following:

    A. *"That's not true."*

    B. *"I didn't say that."*

    C. *"You don't know what you're talking about."*

4. *Stonewalling.* The fourth horseman in Gottman's research is stonewalling, which occurs when the listener withdraws from the interaction, refusing to discuss an issue. This, of course, creates another barrier to being able to talk about a problem constructively, leading to greater distance and animosity.

Any one of these patterns alone can sabotage a marriage. What if there are multiple issues? If one issue leads to another, very serious problems will occur.

WE'RE ALL IN TROUBLE

So look around. Kevin and Stacy are a typical couple; they don't have severe marital issues, but they are in real trouble, and their trouble is not unusual. Again, love and marriage are difficult. Problems can feel and become overwhelming, and many, many couples are feeling these problems.

Do you remember the story of the frog in the kettle? As the story goes, if you throw a frog in boiling water, it will leap out to safety. However, if you put a frog in tepid water and turn the temperature up one degree at a time, the frog will not notice the changes and will eventually boil to death.

This is exactly what I see happening to couples. Small problems that are ignored become moderate-sized ones, and if they're still not addressed, they become horrendous issues. Just like the rising water temperature that killed the frog, problems building one degree at a time are often ignored until it is too late. Living with denial and minimization, justifications, excuses, and rationalizations, is it any wonder many couples refusing to really face issues, refusing to seek effective counsel, end up with very fractured relationships?

This truth was illustrated to me a number of years ago. I had just written a book, and my publishing company sent me on a speaking tour. I was anxious as I prepared to meet with famous people, with large personalities. I anticipated meeting people who had it all together.

I was shocked when after the first interview, with cameras and sound turned off, I was asked to offer advice on a marriage that had gone far astray. In a way, I was relieved to discover again that all of us are capable of allowing small problems to become big, and big problems to become even bigger.

Even those with so much going for them were capable of engaging in self-defeating actions, sabotaging their marriages. In spite of our deep desire for connection, we simply don't have the skills required to solve serious problems. Armed only with the good intentions we had at the altar, we discover they won't carry us very far.

I have come to realize a profound truth: *we all need help*. Some people are better than others at hiding their distress, but we all need help. Some are experts at *denying* their distress, compartmentalizing their issues because *the show must go on*, but we all need help. In spite of how it may seem, there are many, many marriages in trouble.

> SOME PEOPLE ARE EXPERTS
> AT DENYING THEIR DISTRESS,
> COMPARTMENTALIZING THEIR
> ISSUES BECAUSE THE SHOW MUST
> GO ON, BUT WE ALL NEED HELP.

WE ALL NEED HELP

Perhaps you can now see that there is no need to minimize problems. Suffering alone and in silence is a choice you make.

It's really true that in one way or another, we do all need help. But first, we must start with the premise that we're all under-trained and ill-prepared, feel undeserving, and, perhaps the biggest obstacle, have no idea how to really access help.

It's time for all of us to stop hiding in shame, withdrawing in silence, or struggling alone to cope with the immense challenges of love and marriage. Arriving at the belief and understanding that *we all need help*, and admitting that marriage is difficult, is actually quite freeing. When you stop your isolation and fully understand that marriage itself is difficult, you are in a place to receive help.

When a couple embraces the need for ongoing instruction, counseling, and coaching, they've made a giant leap toward finding solutions.

To get to that point, you must embrace these premises:

+ Marriage is difficult.

+ There's no shame in seeking help.

+ Getting help is not easy.

- Getting the right help is even more challenging.
- Getting good help *is* possible.

Now, peruse that list again. Can you embrace these truths? Can you see the work that needs to be done? Can you embrace that we do not enter into love and marriage equipped to handle the challenges?

UNPREPARED!

Yes, love and marriage are hard work. Facing issues you were ill-equipped to handle, you discovered you were in over your head. It's no wonder you, and many, many others, feel unprepared for relationship challenges.

Not only are we overwhelmed with the challenges of marriage, but too often, we settle for too little assistance. Seeking a little bit of help sometimes leaves a couple with a false sense that they have accomplished more than they have. A little bit of help typically renders a small opportunity for change.

Having received only a small degree of help, with a small degree of change, a couple is left vulnerable to sliding back into old patterns of behavior. Many seek and receive the least amount of help possible. The problem is bigger than we think. The work of marriage is more complex than we think.

Can you see the problem?

Many believe the challenges of marriage *shouldn't* be that difficult, and subsequently are not likely to reach out for help. This is a big problem.

Many may admit that marriage is difficult, but don't believe they contribute to those problems. Consequently, they're not likely to reach out for help. This now becomes an even bigger problem.

Many believe it is a mark of shame to reach out for help, making them even more reluctant to seek help. Now we have an even greater problem.

Couples cannot handle all of their marriage issues on their own. It's just not possible. At one time or another, we all need expert guidance. Our best thinking, remember, got us where we are. We are not equipped to handle our own issues.

Marriage is difficult. Just as we need a doctor for medical issues, a dentist for dental issues, and an attorney for legal issues, we all need to give ourselves permission to seek expert marriage help.

In one way or another, both partners contribute to the marriage challenges. Believing the marriage issues are all the result of one person is almost always distorted thinking. Whether you started the problem or only participate in it in some way, both you and your spouse need assistance. It is no shame to ask for help.

THE WORK OF LOVE AND MARRIAGE

I like to think of a marriage as a laboratory where we practice being human, in a positive way. It is here, in my marriage, with my partner, that I see myself in ways that cannot occur in any other setting.

While we may pride ourselves in thinking, "I don't have these problems anywhere else, with anyone else," this actually means very little. Work relationships and friendships have little in comparison to the challenges of marriage.

The work of love and marriage is difficult. It *is* work. I know this goes against our childhood fantasies of finding the *perfect person*, our *soul mate* with whom love and marriage are easy, but it's true. Sure, it's easy during that first romantic date. It's easy for the first few outings. After that, the real work of love and growing your marriage begins.

LOVE IS EASY DURING THAT FIRST ROMANTIC DATE. IT'S EASY FOR THE FIRST FEW OUTINGS. AFTER THAT, THE REAL WORK OF LOVE AND GROWING YOUR MARRIAGE BEGINS.

I was going to learn Spanish. I've tried videos, CDs, and in-class instruction. While I would still like to learn Spanish, my motivation does not exceed the challenges of learning.

Much more recently, I endeavored to learn a minuet on the piano, trying to equal the skills of my twelve-year-old grandson. He practices fifty-five minutes a day; I practice thirty-five minutes a day. I do not have a twelve-year-old sponge for a brain like he does, so big hopes and half-hearted endeavors don't work.

You have your own version of this story. You have started and stopped certain activities with the best of intentions. You were sincere at the start, and then life got in the way. Or to be more honest, something or some things were more important. You weren't as dedicated to losing weight, learning that foreign language, taking that college class, or improving your marriage as you thought.

Our desire to learn Spanish or play a minuet is a bit like our desire to have a vibrant marriage. We're often passive in our approach to the issue—and less than honest. We might even be lazy. We want love to come to us, wrapped in a nice neat package ready to be opened. All we have to do is show up, open the package, and poof! Love in a package just like Spanish on a CD.

It takes more!

CLOSING THOUGHTS

I still think marriage is wonderful, even though that is where all of my idiosyncrasies and character flaws are exposed. I still believe in buying CDs and playing minuets. I still believe in buying travel guides to far-off countries and wistfully listening to Beethoven being played by a twelve-year-old.

I still smile at romantic comedies and chuckle when two unlikely lovers find their way to each other. I still cry in my work when two people ask for help, humbly sit with me, and receive my help, and in so doing, find a way to set differences aside, make repairs to their broken relationship, and smile at the progress they made in finding their way back to each other.

I'm a believer in love and marriage.

I'm also a believer in the work it takes to identify and combat self-defeating, relationship-defeating traits and cultivating those relationship-building skills that hold a couple together.

So, let's believe together that enduring, heart-palpitating love is possible, that the vows we made at the altar were meaningful but must be grounded in the reality that we need more. In the next chapter, we will learn more about why marriages fail.

PRELUDE:
MARK AND CATHY

Mark and Cathy wed after both previously experienced a failed marriage. After a time of being single and having mixed experiences with dating, they met online, dated for a year, and married. Both entered their second marriage with a mixture of excitement and trepidation. Both worried they still carried baggage from their previous marriage.

Both Mark and Cathy vowed inwardly not to repeat patterns and issues from the first time around. However, they soon discovered that problematic character traits follow us like a shadow.

"We both came out of difficult first marriages," Cathy shared during their first counseling session. "I waited several years after my divorce before even dating. My marriage was horrible and the divorce was rough, too. My ex has an alcohol problem and we fought constantly. I sure didn't want to repeat that experience."

She paused, looking over at Mark.

"Mark doesn't have alcohol problems, but he has other issues. I didn't think they were anything I wasn't ready for, but maybe I am the most gullible, codependent woman on the planet. I don't know, but I do know I am still angry at my ex and I don't feel very warm toward my husband either.

"Mark and I took our time getting to know each other," she continued, quickly glancing at Mark, "and I really thought everything would be different this time. Mark's so gentle and kind, at least most of the time. I thought he was my soul mate. I had high hopes and high expectations during the first six months of our marriage, but it's been downhill since then."

"Well, it hasn't been that easy for me either," Mark said sarcastically. "I didn't wait as long as Cathy after my divorce, but we dated for a year before getting married. I thought we knew each other, but there have been a *lot* of surprises."

"Okay," I said, "tell me about these surprises and the problems that have cropped up. I'd also like to hear what steps you've taken to find solutions to them."

I was anxious to see how they would describe their problems and whether either would take ownership for the troubling habits they had brought into their marriage. I needed to see how much insight they had and what steps they had taken to rectify their issues.

"You go first," Mark said.

Cathy shook her head.

"Fine, I'll start," he said. "I'm not the typical man. I'm the one always wanting to go to counseling, but Cathy resists. I wanted to tackle our problems head-on. I want to discuss issues, but she won't. She's got her head in the sand, just like in her first marriage."

Cathy shook her head. I could see she was fighting back tears.

"What?" Mark interrupted.

"That's not fair," she said. "I've resisted going to someone you chose and then you telling the situation from your perspective, blaming everything on me. You're overbearing and I never get a word in. You badger me to go to counseling. You badger me to 'own my stuff' and are constantly telling me 'It takes two to tango.' You always paint me as the bad guy and I'm not up for that. This is a stretch for me to be here today."

"That is not true. I disagree," Mark said firmly. "You can share anything you want and I'll listen to what Dr. Hawkins has to say."

"I hope that is the case, but I don't trust you," Cathy said sharply. "Every time I bring a problem to you, you flip it back onto me. You act like a lawyer and I never feel heard. You find plenty of fault with me but never seem to find fault with yourself. I've never heard you take ownership for any of our problems."

"I can see that we have our work cut out for us, folks," I said. "I'm curious, how much counseling have you done and how useful has it been to you?"

"Well," Cathy began, "you can probably figure out how useful it's been. We've gone to two or three counselors and each time, it's gone poorly. Mark isn't really open for change and seems to need to paint me out as the bad guy. So, I have always refused to go after a couple of sessions. I'm telling you this from my heart: If this counseling doesn't work, I might be done with the marriage."

In only a few minutes, Mark and Cathy revealed that they had tremendous distrust toward one another. They exhibited a great deal of resentment and pain. On a positive note, however, they had agreed to try counseling one more time. I had my work cut out for me—and so did they.

WHY MARRIAGES FAIL

I will reveal to you a love potion, without medicine, without herbs,
without any witch's magic; if you want to be loved, then love.
—Hecaton of Rhodes

Failure is such a strong word. A rather ugly word, if you ask me. It might have been better to use a different word, but "failure" is really the correct word.

Failure typically means falling short of a certain standard, like receiving a very poor grade on a test. That's one kind of failure—failing to adequately prepare, failing to study properly, and failing to really take the class and impending exam seriously.

I remember another time when I failed to obey the laws of the road and chose to ride my motorcycle before my sixteenth birthday. I was appropriately pulled over by police, given a citation, and forced to apply for my license three months *after* my sixteenth birthday. This was a failure to follow the law.

But a failed marriage is far more complex. It's not as straightforward as a failed exam or failing to follow guidelines for driving. A failed marriage is not an event but a process—often a long, slow process. Like metal left out in salty air by the ocean, disintegrating over time, a marriage disintegrates when not cared for properly. It's a slow, gradual, incessant disintegration.

> **A FAILED MARRIAGE IS NOT AN EVENT BUT A PROCESS. IT'S AN ACCUMULATION OF MANY TROUBLING EVENTS THAT TAKE A HORRENDOUS TOLL ON A COUPLE'S RELATIONSHIP.**

A failed marriage is an accumulation of many troubling events that take a horrendous toll on a couple's relationship. This is why it is hard to predict failure in the early days of the marriage. It's like a slow leak in a dam that finally, with enough stress, fractures and breaks.

REFLECTIONS OF A FAILING MARRIAGE

"I was so sure our marriage would work," Cathy said softly. "In the beginning, I was careful, cautious, even guarded. I just knew this time was going to be different."

Cathy went on explain how when she first felt problems developing in her marriage, she distracted herself from the pain with "the daily activities of life." This denial kept her from making any changes. She shared how she became involved with her daughter's sports and piano lessons, church groups, and so many volunteer activities.

"All of these kept me from confronting Mark," she said. "And if I ever did force an issue with Mark, I ended up feeling bad about myself.

"I remember the first time he blew up at my girls," she continued. "I was shocked, but he turned it back on me. He said I was overreacting. That was how all our confrontation went."

"So, you saw some red flags," I said.

"Yes," she answered, "but how could I be sure it wasn't me? He told me I was overprotective. Too sensitive. I thought he might be right."

"What changed?" I asked.

"I couldn't tolerate the tension anymore. I was scared to say anything for fear of his reprisal," she said. "Our arguments got more hostile. I finally lost it and knew I had to create some space between us so I could clear my head. I asked Mark to leave a few weeks ago."

"Was there one event that really created a need for a separation?" I asked.

"No, not really," she said. "I've been thinking about it for a long time now. It wasn't a onetime decision. It was a lot of little things. I'd started planning in my head how I was going to get out and began sharing with a friend who gave me strength. Maybe one of our bigger fights tipped things, when he really hurt my feelings. I thought about how much life I had left and decided I was better off alone than with him."

This may all sound drastic to you. You might think this is an unusual situation. It's not. You might think this woman is in more turmoil than the average woman. She's not. Counseling couples in conflict is my profession, so you might think I'm exaggerating the problem. I'm not.

You might also wonder why I chose to cite a woman's perspective. I could quote men just as easily. A high percentage of men are suffering in silence too. They didn't think they would end up like this, lonely and feeling misunderstood, desperate to be appreciated and cared for. They feel cheated, working hard to provide for the family and having the sense that they are getting too little in return.

A LONG, SLOW DEATH

You can see that marriage failure isn't an event but a slow, drawn-out process. As with the story of Cathy and Mark, it is rarely due to one incident. Most marriages have really ended long before the spouses part ways.

Oh, you might say, "It was the straw that broke the camel's back," and so perhaps the failure appeared to be an event, but marriage failures typically are anything but one mishap. Marriage failure is a slow, painful deterioration.

Is it fair to compare a marriage failure to a death? I think so. When we look back at most marriage failures, we can see the signs of disintegration. If we look closely and critically, we can see all the symptoms that led to marriage failure.

In the past few years, my wife and I have watched the decline of our parents. As our parents ultimately passed away, it was after a slow, arduous struggle to hang on to vestiges of life. Elderly parents often grapple heroically with one health issue after another, struggling to hold on to some positive aspect of life. The children do the best they can to help the parents make wise decisions, but they know the end is coming.

Perhaps marriages in desperate trouble are something like that: holding on to small vestiges of a relationship that perhaps they thought was healthy but wasn't, hoping beyond hope that something fortuitous will occur to bring vibrancy back to the marriage. This, in many cases, is the height of denial. This is often magical thinking.

Am I suggesting these couples abandon their efforts and call it quits earlier? Absolutely not. Is marriage failure inevitable? Of course not. However, if a marriage is in serious trouble, and if significant steps are not taken to stop the erosion of vibrancy and health in the marriage, then yes, death is inevitable.

STATISTICS

Marriages fail. We know this. Marriages fail for different reasons, but sometimes couples are so blinded by the factors leading up to divorce they say they didn't see it coming.

When we step back and critically review marriages in trouble, we can see some alarming statistics. While they never tell the whole story, they can give us a stern and realistic perspective on what is happening.

You're likely aware of the dismal statistics on marriage, though most people don't talk about them. Here are the latest facts: nearly 50 percent of first marriages fail. Second marriages fare a bit worse, with nearly 60 percent ending in divorce. Third marriages fail at nearly 70 percent.

These are tough odds. We would rarely risk any venture if we thought we had only a 30, 40, or 50 percent chance of success. Yet that's exactly what we face when we enter into a marriage.

THE STRAINS OF MARRIAGE

The statistics suggest marriage is a risky endeavor. Anyone who has been married can attest to its many challenges. There is no other relationship that compares to marriage in any way. It is unique in its demands and its benefits. In fact, I don't know if anyone can truly understand the unique stresses of marriage without experiencing it firsthand. It is that unique, that challenging, and that difficult to navigate.

It is not uncommon for me to hear someone say, "I don't have problems like this in my other relationships." Is this actually true? Maybe, maybe not.

You are not likely to feel the same challenges in your friendships that you do in marriage. The two relationships are *completely* different. Consider you live with your mate, day in and day out. Consider that your moods, highs and lows, are seen day and night by your mate but rarely by friends and associates. Others don't stress you the way your mate does, and they probably never or rarely see *shadow side functioning* experienced by you and your mate.

Think about this. Friends and associates are not likely to see your foul moods, your temper outbursts, your selfishness. They may never see you on your worst day. Your mate does.

It is the cumulation of all the stresses and strains of marriage, and the failure to resolve them, that contributes to the decline of a marriage. Now let's consider specific issues leading to its failure.

> **FRIENDS AND ASSOCIATES ARE NOT LIKELY TO SEE YOUR FOUL MOODS, YOUR TEMPER OUTBURSTS, OR YOUR SELFISHNESS. THEY MAY NEVER SEE YOU ON YOUR WORST DAY. YOUR MATE DOES.**

FACTORS IN A FAILING MARRIAGE

Having sat with countless couples over countless hours of navigating conflict, I know there are common themes. What are some common denominators for couples finding themselves in desperate straits?

1. Fighting About Anything

As you might imagine, I've been asked what couples fight about. For years, I gave the standard answers: money, sex, children, in-laws. And that is all true. But my answer now is much broader than that. In fact, my answer now is *anything. Couples fight about anything and everything!*

How can I make such a statement? Because it's true. Once a certain threshold of intolerance and irritability has been reached, goodwill erodes until it's nearly absent and the fun's evaporated. At this point, it's easy for couples to fight about *anything.*

I remember an embarrassing incident in my marriage about ten years ago. I flew into Seattle-Tacoma International Airport on a Sunday night, arriving home at around eleven o'clock. I just wanted to go to bed, but I had some work yet to do to prepare for Monday morning. The incident, *as I recall it*, went something like this:

I walked in the door and saw the peanut butter jar on the counter, lid off.

"Why is the peanut butter sitting on the counter with the lid off?" I asked critically.

"David," Christie said patiently, "you're tired from a long flight. We really don't need to fight about the peanut butter."

"I'm not fighting," I persisted. "I just want to know why the peanut butter is open on the counter. Why didn't you put the peanut butter away?"

Christie accurately perceived my tiredness and irritability and thankfully refused to bite. "David," she continued, becoming exasperated herself, "I'm glad you're home. Let's discuss this in the morning if it's still bothering you. I'm not going to fight with you about this."

I groused a bit more, muttering something about peanut butter on the counter before going to bed! You see, we are capable of fighting about *anything*.

Another case in point: a couple came to their most recent appointment just after a fight. This is not an uncommon occurrence.

"What happened?" I asked.

"I asked him how he liked my new sundress and he said I looked like an old woman in it," she said.

"I didn't say that," he snapped back.

"Well," she continued, "that's what you meant."

"I said that it looks like an older woman's dress," he said.

And so it goes.

Was the issue really the dress or the way he shared his opinion? However you look at this situation, you can see that a couple in distress can fight about *anything*.

2. The Process Is the Problem

Marriages also fail because couples not only fight about anything, but the way they fight about an issue *never* leads to resolution.

Far too many couples are engaged in constant conflict. This is not often seen by friends and family because most couples choose to *put on a good appearance.* Yet, behind closed doors, it's a different story. In the privacy of their homes, they fight about anything and everything; their relationship becomes marked and marred by conflict.

With couples in distress, it's important to recognize that the *issues* are not really the issue—rather, the process is the problem. The process of not resolving issues is what leads to marriage failure.

What do I mean by that? While there might be one or two *hot spots* in a relationship, the central issue is that most of us do not have the skills to truly resolve issues. Subsequently, *any* concern becomes a *major* concern. What one couple might consider trivial, another couple is willing to continue fighting about for hours. Spouses withdraw from one another, often spending days in silence.

I have studied many couples who were unable, and sometimes unwilling, to let an issue go. I have spent a great deal of time exploring the dynamics of couples locked in power struggles, willing to fight, flee, or freeze at any upset.

Common Traits of Contentious Couples

What are some common traits of couples locked in cold or hot wars?

+ *Couples locked into oppositional stances*—viewing their mate as *the enemy* and someone they should fight, not knowing how to foster collaboration.

+ *Couples frequently angry with one another*—failing to manage emotions, becoming angry, passive-aggressive, and failing to think straight.

+ *Couples with poor conflict-resolution/communication skills*—inability to stay issue-focused, share feelings, and speak respectfully.

+ *Couples with poor impulse control*—unable to talk about one issue at a time, manage emotions, and be solution-focused.

+ *Couples using reprisal for talking openly about concerns*—exhibiting an inability to tolerate or consider concerns of their mate.

+ *Couples with a tendency to blame and fault-find*—viewing the actions of their mate in critical, negative ways, assigning hurtful motives, and behaving in ways they believe they never do.

+ *Couples who express rigidly held beliefs about the other*—unable to view their mate positively and flexibly, unable to alter perspective or consider their mate's strengths.

+ *Couples who offer little insight into their contribution to their problems*—unable to see their role in problems or monitor their actions.

+ *Couples who do not recognize these destructive patterns*—unable and perhaps unwilling to acknowledge wrongdoing, they minimize their issues and blame their mate for them, further reinforcing the ongoing conflict.

Can you see the enormous challenges inherent in marriage and the many, many ways couples can veer off course? Any one of these issues is enough to cause significant problems. What if there are several of these patterns of relating present? Can you see how difficult it is to maintain a healthy, loving connection to another person? The problems cited above are common and can lead to horrific challenges for couples.

3. Refusal to Take Responsibility

It is important to say more about the issue of refusing to take responsibility for the harm one does in a marriage. This is a most serious and significant issue because without full acceptance of harm done, the wounds fester. The wounded one adapts to the harm but remains internally wounded. This becomes a place where resentment builds.

By not accepting responsibility, the one who has done the harm doesn't change. They minimize, rationalize, or deny their actions, rendering themselves fully capable of harming in the same way again. This adds a huge barrier to a couple's efforts to overcome their challenges.

While most of us give assent to the importance of *taking responsibility for hurtful actions*, it might surprise you to hear most couples are notoriously bad at owning up to them, acknowledging harm done, and making repairs.

Recently, a man came to see me who was angry, irritable, and depressed. His wife had urged him to get help because his moods were causing problems for her and their children.

As I heard more of his story, it became apparent that he was coping with his depression by gambling, an effort by him to create some positive feelings in his otherwise boring and depressing life.

As we explored his behavior, it became apparent that there was a lot more to his story. He was caught in a vicious cycle: he would lose money on gambling, feel guilty and ashamed, and hide the gambling from his wife. His gambling became an addiction that worsened his mood and temperament.

His wife had recently discovered the gambling and deception, felt understandably furious and betrayed, and confronted him. It went poorly. In an effort at self-preservation, he blamed his wife for *snooping* and discovering his gambling. He minimized his own actions and subsequent deceit. She became even more distrusting, and the issue grew to the point where resolution seemed to be impossible.

There is now a cancer in their marriage. Remember that refusal to take responsibility causes *huge* problems in a marriage. His gambling, deception, and blame-shifting created enormous problems in their relationship. His refusal to take responsibility for his addiction led to an even greater loss of trust and a downward spiral for him, his wife, and their marriage.

If this situation occurred once in the lifetime of a marriage, it could probably survive. The conflict could actually be an opportunity for deeper and healthier connection. However, if one deceit is layered upon another, one blame-shift layered on another blame-shift, one lack of true remorse and reparation layered upon another lack of remorse and reparation, any marriage will be in deep trouble.

TRUST AND TRANSPARENCY ARE NECESSARY INGREDIENTS FOR ANY RELATIONSHIP TO SURVIVE; WITHOUT THEM, ANY MARRIAGE WILL SUFFER.

When trust and transparency are missing, intimacy is impossible. These are necessary ingredients for any relationship to survive; without them, any marriage will suffer.

4. Lack of Preparation

Another reason for marriage failure is that couples simply aren't mentally or emotionally prepared for the rigors of two becoming one. Remember, we've said love and marriage are hard work and require much focus and attention.

How can a lack of preparation be a problem? Perhaps, as you reflect on your own marriage, you can think about where and when you were prepared with the following mandatory skills for being a good spouse:

- *Active, attentive, compassionate listening.* We are unprepared because we haven't been taught these skills, and if we are fortunate enough to have some of them, we likely *caught* them from caring parents rather than being *taught* them.

- *Owning our part in a problem.* We are unprepared to admit that we contributed to the issue. If we are fortunate enough to have learned this skill, it was likely from a series of negative experiences.

- *Validating another's experience.* We are unprepared to accept, support, and affirm our mate's experience, which leaves them feeling alone and unheard.

- *Sharing feelings, our own and our mate's.* We are unprepared to share our own feelings and those of our mate. This skill is only learned in a healthy family environment or in our relationships.

+ *Effective problem-solving.* We are unprepared to give up any need to be right, being flexible and giving, caring more for the relationship than our own personal satisfaction.

As you can see, most couples have an enormous gap in their skills, leaving them unprepared for the rigors and hard work of marriage. These are *basic* skills that are nearly always lacking in all but the most mature marriages. This leads to very serious problems. It is no wonder that so many complain about their lack of preparation for being in a healthy relationship. Marriage is hard work, and missing any of these skills will lead to trouble and increase the likelihood that the marriage will fail.

SIGNS AND SYMPTOMS OF A MARRIAGE IN TROUBLE

We know a lot about why marriages fail. When reviewing failing marriages, we discover similarities. While couples fail in many different ways, certain patterns emerge. What are these patterns?

One of the most common patterns I have found is the failure of a couple to see their marriage as a *renewable* relationship. By this, I mean that any couple—in fact *every* couple—is capable of being in relational trouble if they are not always on their toes, ever on the lookout for ways their marriage could fail. There is no coasting, no time when they can sit back and say, "We made it."

> WHEN A COUPLE FAILS TO SEE THEIR MARRIAGE AS A RENEWABLE RELATIONSHIP, THEY LOSE SIGHT OF THE FACT THAT THEY MUST CONTINUE TO BUILD INTIMACY AND CONNECTION.

Most couples forget this truth, selfishly expecting their mate to continue to meet their needs in the same ways they did at the start of their relationship. Feeling entitled to intimacy and connection, most lose sight of the fact that they must build this into their marriage continuously. However, this takes preparation.

Since this doesn't happen automatically, many couples feel profoundly disappointed. They look at their mate and ask, silently or out loud, "What in the world has happened? Why are you not still meeting my needs? Why are you not still my princess or knight in shining armor?"

Couples in trouble feel jilted, betrayed, and angry. Out of this deeply disappointed place, they begin having more and more symptoms of a couple in distress. Built-up resentments and intimacies gone cold are all ingredients for trouble in a relationship.

What are some of the symptoms and issues of couples who have lost their way and are now heading for serious trouble? In an article titled "The Most Common Marriage Problems That Arise After 10 Years Together,"[5] Kelsey Borresen describes the following eight issues:

1. *Couples start feeling more like roommates than romantic partners.* Couples stop engaging in *date nights* and are simply engaged in the tasks of raising children and earning money to pay the bills. They've forgotten about the importance of keeping romance a part of their marriage.

2. *Couples become bored with their lives together.* Many individuals in marriage slip into being boring people. They fail to create adventure. They slip into monotonous lifestyles, failing to share new dreams, goals, and ideas.

3. *Couples' sex lives have faded.* Too many couples' sex lives fade over time, often without discussion or appropriate attention. These couples have become bored, failing to explore new and creative sexual activities together.

---

5. Kelsey Borresen, "The Most Common Marriage Problems That Arise After 10 Years Together," *The Huffington Post*, January 2, 2019 (www.huffpost.com/entry/marriage-problems-solutions-10-years_n_5c2a4a80e4b08aaf7a92bcfb).

4. *Couples feel dissatisfied because they think marriage has prevented them from accomplishing certain life goals.* Couples naturally make sacrifices when it comes to raising a family, or buying and caring for a home; as a result, sometimes other dreams and goals are forgotten. Failing to continually renegotiate their relationship and renegotiate their goals, they end up in trouble.

5. *Couples' tolerance for one another has dissipated.* In the beginning, your mate could do no wrong. Not surprisingly, the rose-colored glasses you viewed your mate through in the beginning faded, and reality sets in. Failing to resolve resentments that naturally seep into the relationship, tolerances for the foibles of their mate's character having declined, they end up in trouble.

6. *Couples stop celebrating milestones, big and small.* As time goes on, it is tempting to forget to celebrate the small and large milestones. Couples in trouble fail to weave celebrations into their marriage as a way to counterbalance the challenges that are part of a relationship.

7. *Couples forget how to be goofy and have fun.* Couples in trouble have forgotten to keep life exciting, forgetting how to be childlike and have fun. Couples in trouble have failed to keep a relationship fresh by maintaining a playfulness with each other.

8. *Couples become stressed over being homeowners.* In too many cases, the thrill of home ownership turns into the drudgery of rebuilding the deck, mowing the lawn, and replacing the roof, not to mention repairing or replacing appliances that have started to wear out. Failing to maintain a balance of responsibilities with the joys of home ownership leads to a couple being in trouble.

In a way, marriage is just a series of problems. Marriages fail when problem after unresolved problem becomes insurmountable. Couples in trouble fail to prepare for challenges and then fail to resolve them when they occur, leading to even greater issues. We can see again that love and marriage take incredible work, and if that work is not done, the marriage will end in failure.

COUPLES STILL CHOOSE MARRIAGE

One might think that with all the problems couples face, many people would opt out of marriage, but that is not the case. You might think with all the potential problems, couples might shy away from marriage, but they still choose marriage, time and again.

Let's remind ourselves why couples choose marriage and why it's important for us to keep this in mind. Even after being wounded, perhaps even betrayed and hurt, couples still gravitate to love. Even with the odds stacked against them, couples choose connection.

In an article titled "8 Facts About Love and Marriage in America,"[6] authors A. W. Geiger and Gretchen Livingston cite the following reasons, in order of importance, for getting married:

+ Love

+ Making a lifelong commitment

+ Companionship

+ Having children

+ A relationship recognized in a religious ceremony

+ Financial stability

+ Legal rights and benefits

So, for various reasons, people still choose marriage. Most people will get married. What can we say about this? Perhaps we don't say enough about the importance and power of love, the power that causes couples to face the odds and take the chance of having a healthy, loving relationship. Even though they are naive and unskilled as well as unprepared, and the challenges are enormous, couples take the risk. The question is how to help them take this risk in a more informed way.

Even though love and marriage are difficult, even with all of the struggles and reasons marriages fail, even after all of this, I still believe in love. I still believe in marriage and believe we can all become better equipped to face the challenges of marriage more effectively.

6. A. W. Geiger and Gretchen Livingston, "8 Facts About Love and Marriage in America," Pew Research Center, February 13, 2019 (www.pewresearch.org/fact-tank/2019/02/13/8-facts-about-love-and-marriage).

I'm a believer in love.

I'm also a believer in the work it takes to identify and work on self-defeating, relationship-defeating traits and cultivating those relationship building skills that hold a couple together.

Are you ready to learn more about what makes a marriage fail and how to make marriage counseling work for you? I can help you get there.

PRELUDE: CYNTHIA AND JACK

"I want you out, Jack!" Cynthia yelled. "I'm done. I don't want to live like this anymore. It's over."

"Are you serious?" Jack yelled back. "You're kicking me out because of one night with my buddies? You've got to be kidding."

"Jack, c'mon," Cynthia said. "It's not just your buddies. It's your drinking, your lies about your drinking, your broken promises. I'm sick of your excuses, your promises, your so-called commitments. It's so much more than one night with your buddies. I can't live like this anymore."

"Live like what?" he said. "Like living in your dream house? Like driving your new Lexus? Like tennis at the club?"

"Jack," Cynthia said with exasperation. "You're not listening to me. You're not hearing me. I'm out of breath. I'm out of words. I'm out of caring. I'm not going to spend another day of my life trying to make you understand. Leave. Now. Please."

Jack turned and walked out of the house, slamming the door. His heart was racing, his head was raging. Moments later, he stormed back into their living room.

"You're not going to do this, Cynthia, throwing away twelve years of our lives over one bad night," he said. "You are ruining our lives, our kids' lives, our families. I'm not going to sit by while you blow everything out of proportion."

Cynthia stared at Jack in silence.

"I can't believe what you're saying, Jack," she finally said. "This is not about one bad night. This is about years and years of me feeling unheard. Years and years of you working too hard, playing too hard, drinking too much. Years and years of me feeling like I don't matter. I'm done, Jack."

"Well, I'm not," he said.

"I'm done, Jack, and I want you out," she said. "I've already contacted an attorney. I'm considering divorce. I'm really done. I'm done, Jack."

"An attorney?" Jack shouted. "Without even talking to me? Without even giving me a chance to get my drinking under control? That is really low, Cynthia."

"C'mon, Jack," Cynthia said. "I told you I wanted a separation over a year ago. I brought it up again two months ago when you got angry and left and didn't come back for six hours. Don't you remember that? This isn't a sudden thing. Our marriage has been dying for years. It's time to bury the body."

Jack moved toward the door, then turned back to Cynthia. "You do what you've got to do, but I'm not going along with this." Jack slammed the door.

Cynthia heard him start his truck, his tires spitting gravel as he left their driveway. She stared out the window, watching his taillights as he sped away.

Cynthia sank down in her chair, motionless for a few moments. All of her fears, hopes, and dreams, as well as her feelings of immense loss, flooded in as she began to cry. She felt sad, angry, hurt, hopeless. She began sobbing as she clutched her head in her hands.

I hate him, she thought, alone in the silence of the room. *Why did it have to come to this? I've tried to make this work, again and again and again!*

She pulled her knees to her chest, reflecting on the many times she had been in fights like this one—Jack being angry, making demands, not listening. She pulled her knees closer and cried. Her dreams of a happy, loving marriage were gone. She began to worry about her future, but that was too much to think about now.

She let out a deep sigh, still clutching her knees. The room was eerily quiet. Feeling alone and overwhelmed, she knew her marriage was over. Their marriage had failed.

AUTOPSY OF A
FAILED MARRIAGE

*Relationships fail because people take their own insecurities
and try and twist them into their partner's flaws.*
—Baylor Barbee

Does it sound sensational to use the word *autopsy* in describing a marriage failure? Maybe. Yet, ask those who have experienced such a loss, and they are likely to use the words *failure, tragic ending,* or even *death.*

There is no easy way to talk about the chasm between the idealized hopefulness of a new marriage and the stark reality of a marriage ending. There are no words to adequately convey what happens when one's hopes, wishes, and dreams have been utterly dashed, replaced by significant loss.

But a marriage failure doesn't just happen. In fact, the deterioration of a marriage goes through identifiable stages, from the idealization of a new relationship and the hopefulness of building dreams together, to the disillusionment, detachment, and ultimate failure of a marriage.

How does so much hopefulness end in such tragedy? Let's look closer at how this happens.

IDEALIZATION

We have explored the naivete of *the honeymoon phase*, also known as idealization, an idyll time of glamour and fascination with one another. This is a time of intense romantic love, a time when we attribute overly positive qualities to another person. This season of a relationship is marked by intense feelings of ecstasy and longing for the other person.

Idealization is actually an important phase in a relationship. It is a time of feeling overly close to our mate, desiring to be with them. We notice all of their positive qualities and barely notice the negative ones. Few enter a relationship with an honest grasp of its inherent problems. If we didn't overestimate our mate's virtues, we might not proceed in the relationship.

During the idealization phase, everything about the other person seems right, even unbelievable. This perfect individual can do no wrong. In fact, it is common to hear someone describe their loved one as "too good to be true," "soul mate," and "perfect" during this phase.

The phase of idealization is also fueled by biochemistry, with hormones such as oxytocin, dopamine, and serotonin causing us to be partially blinded to the real dangers in the relationship. We don't feel good just because the relationship is going so smoothly. We literally feel good because of the hormones. Lightheaded, we obsess about being with this other person all the time.

However, this euphoric feeling and those feel-good hormones don't usually last. Research indicates that the intense loving feelings of the honeymoon phase lasts six to eighteen months before wearing off and wearing out.

Jack and Cynthia did not have a rush of feel-good hormones at the start of their relationship. It was not love at first sight, nor did they fall madly in love when they first met in high school, where they sang together in the choir. They hung out together in a group, but nothing more.

After graduation, Jack joined the U.S. Army, while Cynthia went off to college, studying to become a nurse. Home from school and on leave, they met again at a friend's house. They enjoyed catching up. He shared some of the rigors of army life, while she shared the excitement of being away at college.

This encounter was quite different from their experiences in high school. This time, there *was* some intense infatuation and some idealization.

Jack found Cynthia lively and exciting, balancing out his shyness. She found his shyness to be attractive, balancing her extroversion. Unlike their friendship in high school, this time, their hormones were sparked.

Young and impetuous, they wanted to spend all their time together, but they had some obstacles to overcome. He would be deployed for several more months and then stationed on the East Coast. Jack wanted Cynthia to move with him to his next assignment. Excited and filled with feel-good hormones, she said she would go anywhere with Jack.

Their intoxication with each other fit many of the traits found in the idealization phase; both saw only the good in the other, leading to a hasty proposal and commitment to marriage.

Their relationship was carried away by their idealization of each other. Idealization, however, has its dangers.

DANGERS OF IDEALIZATION

It is easy to predict the problems that arise from idealizing a mate. Times together are fun-filled and exciting, but they can't last forever. Perceptions are colored by hormones, and they won't last forever either. Dedicated time together will also dissipate. Reality must set in at some point. Remember, this phase of relating is marked by naivete, impulsiveness, and hormones.

Drs. Les and Leslie Parrott, in their article "3 Reasons to Stop Idealizing Your Mate,"[7] say there are three good reasons to be on guard about idealizing a partner:

1. *Idealization leads to unmet expectations.* Expectations built up during the honeymoon phase are often hard for a spouse to live up to and unmet expectations formed in this phase of relating are a major issue in many marriages. Idealizations often become fixed and rigid, leading to unrealistic expectations.

7. Drs. Les and Leslie Parrott, "3 Reasons to Stop Idealizing Your Mate," SYMBIS Assessment, September 9, 2020 (www.symbis.com/blog/3-reasons-to-stop-idealizing-your-spouse).

2. *Idealization leads to dehumanization.* Idealization can lead you to believe your mate can do no wrong—this person becomes super-human in your mind. You assume your mate is perfect and will continue to live up to your unrealistic expectations.

3. *Idealization limits empathy.* Viewing your mate as a perfect person can limit your empathy for them. Focusing on how your mate has let you down when they don't live up to your ideal version of them also creates frustration and anger.

In spite of these dangers, it is nearly impossible to avoid this phase of relating. Getting to know a new partner, creating new dreams together, and building new possibilities, along with a strong dose of hormones, lead to inevitable idealization and then disappointment. Idealization, as exciting as it is, is simply not sustainable.

DREAM BUILDING

After the idealization or honeymoon phase, couples often shift their focus slightly. Talk shifts to everyday practicalities, like where they will live and how involved they will be with each other. While planning a future is still exciting, couples often feel the excitement of the idealization phase begin to fade. They begin exploring together other aspects of their relationship.

This *dream-building phase* is the exploratory time when a couple, in a more levelheaded way, really thinks about the other person and whether their values, lifestyle, dreams, and passions meld together.

This phase is a critical time in a relationship because it is here where values are explored, dreams are shared, and true compatibility is tested. Differences are more closely examined, and couples test their ability to navigate differences and manage conflict. Couples go through a process of determining if the other person really fits into their life.

Imagine that a left-wing Democrat strikes up strong, positive feelings for a right-wing Republican. Perhaps a country girl is deeply attached to a city boy. While these differences may seem trivial at first glance, in the dream-building phase, these and other issues are taken more seriously.

There are significant implications when religious, political, and social preferences, to name a few possible differences, are taken into consideration.

Dream-building is just that—building dreams. Sometimes, there is plenty of chemistry between two people, but their lifestyle issues don't coincide. Perhaps there are plenty of shared values, but the chemistry simply isn't there.

Dream-building is not, of course, only about the couple. Dream-building also often involves one's extended family. How do her parents feel about him? How do his parents feel about her? How do their siblings and extended family feel about their chosen mate? If there has been a previous marriage with children, how do the children feel about him or her?

The complexities of uniting two very different people, from different backgrounds and different values, are extensive. In the idealization phase, no obstacle is insurmountable. In the dream-building phase, things get real. Reality may clash with idealization, and relationships often destabilize, at least for a time.

IN THE IDEALIZATION PHASE, NO OBSTACLE IS INSURMOUNTABLE FOR A COUPLE. IN THE DREAM-BUILDING PHASE, THINGS GET REAL.

Jack and Cynthia tackled a few dream-building challenges immediately. Jack would be stationed at Fort Bragg in North Carolina, and Cynthia discovered she could transfer credits and attend university in nearby Raleigh/Durham. They were excited they so easily overcame these potential obstacles. Not all future obstacles would be managed as easily.

Armed with exciting dreams, Jack and Cynthia began weaving a life together, evaluating each other and their relationship in the process. Things seemed to be meshing for them; now they were overjoyed to finally spend time together. While everything appeared positive for the first six months of their relationship, fueled at first by the longing they had experienced in hopes of seeing each other soon, and perhaps a strong dose of hormones, reality soon invaded their new relationship.

Reality, clashing with idealization, often sparks disillusionment.

DISILLUSIONMENT

Disillusionment is the sinking feeling you get when the ideal you believe you've found in another person is no longer there. It's the feeling of a lovely dream being crushed by a harsh reality. The reality of this person is not quite as shiny as the dream.

No one wants to feel disillusioned. In fact, given the alternative, most of us would rather cling to idealization, optimism, and hopefulness. Couples in this phase of relating often resist facing the realities of the relationship. But magical thinking cannot last.

Everyone knows about this stage in a relationship because everyone has experienced it. Feeling disillusioned is a normal phase. When it comes to marriages beginning to fail, however, a couple can get stuck in constant feelings of discouragement and frustration. Disillusionment can become an entrenched attitude that festers and grows.

It is common, during the phase of disillusionment, to hear spouses say, "I don't know what happened. He (or she) was such a different person," implying that perhaps they had been duped. In addition to feeling disillusioned, the couple often feels confused. It is hard for them to fully grasp what is happening.

Many feel disoriented during this phase. Believing your mate was *someone else* who is now acting in ways you find unfamiliar and concerning leaves you feeling profoundly confused. You wonder, *What is going on? Why is this person not living up to my idealized standards?*

Becoming disillusioned might begin innocently enough: perhaps your mate's quirks no longer seem endearing. In the early stages of the relationship, you overlook their foibles. Perhaps you found her lateness cute, or the way she snorts when she laughs charming. Now these traits are annoying. Her halo starts losing a little of its sparkle.

His daily habits, like the way he combs his hair or how he cleans (or doesn't clean) his car, start to tarnish his shiny suit of armor. Some aspects of the relationship move from cute to annoying to complete disillusionment.

It had to happen, right? Remember, no one can maintain an image of perfection indefinitely. In fact, believing the intoxicating love of early days will last forever makes for an even greater crash. Keeping expectations in perspective, and knowing what to do with little annoyances, is one of the factors predicting whether a couple will make it long term.

It took a while for the glow to fade in Jack and Cynthia's marriage, but it did. Both loved the early days of their relationship, but again, the feel-good hormones didn't last, and reality set in. Mortgages, work, bills, children, and the tedium of daily life began to take a toll on their relationship. The *feel-good*, hormonal period of idealization had worn thin.

When the innocence and naivete of early relationships clash with the starkness of work—and don't forget those little annoyances—disillusionment takes over. Jack was used to army life: regimented, orderly, and predictable. He was not prepared for his wife to challenge how he expected things to be done. His demanding, controlling ways wore thin for Cynthia very quickly.

When Jack gave Cynthia orders on how they would run their home, she had her own crash of reality. She didn't handle her feelings well, either exploding in anger or imploding into depression. Both reactions took a huge toll on their relationship.

Disillusionment, if not confronted and dealt with effectively, or if handled in unhealthy ways, causes spouses to push away from each other. This, of course, leads to an even greater problem: detachment in one form or another.

DETACHMENT

From idealization to dream-building to disillusionment, we move to the state of *detachment*. Detachment can strike a powerful blow to a relationship. If some of the glow of the early days is not maintained, if at least some of the idealization is not kept alive along the way, a couple loses the warmth and connection needed to caringly resolve problems, and a sense of hopelessness often sets in.

RELATIONSHIPS ARE BUILT ON CONNECTION. COUPLES MUST FIND A WAY, EVEN IN THE MIDST OF DISILLUSIONMENT, TO STAY CONNECTED.

Relationships are built on connection. Couples must find a way, even in the midst of disillusionment, to stay connected. They must, in a real sense, form a new relationship that incorporates *some* feelings of disillusionment as well as connection, so that the detachment does not grow. They must normalize the fact that their relationship is not all they hoped it would be, but it will be a *real* relationship.

Think about this: for any couple to sustain positive feelings toward each other, they must have a *love bank* of those positive feelings from which they can draw when times are tough. These memories of better times help couples stay connected and work through the difficult times. When times are challenging, they can always know from past experience that better times are coming.

A healthy couple experiences conflict, to be sure, but they remember the good feelings—their love bank for their mate—and this helps them stay connected. They know and trust their feelings of hurt or even anger will dissipate, and fondness will return. They trust and know the connection is not permanently severed, but only temporarily broken.

When detachment becomes the primary way a couple copes with conflict and hard times, the relationship bridge weakens. Positive memories are not as easily retrieved. When hurt and sadness are the couple's primary feelings, when it's hard to remember past good times, the relationship bridge suffers more damage.

Cynthia felt burdened by her frustration with Jack and began to experience anxiety over the unresolved issues between them. Feeling unheard and dismissed by him, unable to resolve issues, she did what many do—she detached from him.

Jack detached in his own way. He developed a habit of retreating and withdrawing, finding it easier to cope with emotional pain in this way.

When confronted with the idea of detaching, many deny, justify, or minimize their actions. Their detachment may be outside of their awareness, or they may justify their actions, citing withdrawal as a way to cope. This may work for the moment, but it adds more to the destructive stage in a deteriorating marriage.

Cynthia tried to resolve her issues with Jack, but his constant defensiveness and blame-shifting caused her to withdraw from him even further.

Jack felt Cynthia pushing away and became increasingly irritated by it. Detachment, whatever the cause, doesn't feel good to either party, and without skills to resolve the issue and recreate connection, it leads to further problems.

Cynthia wasn't the only one to withdraw; they both withdrew from each other. Like other couples in trouble, Jack and Cynthia coped in destructive ways, creating self-defeating and relationship-defeating patterns. This destructive coping added another layer of problems to their increasing marriage failure.

DESTRUCTIVE COPING

Everyone experiences tension and must find ways to cope with it. Healthy coping involves solving problems and finding ways of alleviating stress until those problems can be resolved.

Destructive coping may alleviate stress and tension temporarily, but it only adds to the layer of serious problems. We see that happening with

Jack and Cynthia—their destructive coping by withdrawing and failing to talk about their issues led to further marriage failure.

Each stage in the deterioration of a relationship can be interrupted, but unfortunately, this seldom happens. Once a relationship begins a downward spiral, the trend often continues, fueled by destructive coping. Detachment, if not decisively interrupted, leads to further, often amplified, destructive coping.

You might think we would notice our destructive coping patterns and stop them, but this rarely happens due to the power of denial. It is well-known that we see weaknesses in another far more readily than we see them in ourselves. As destructive as our actions are, we falsely believe we are coping effectively.

There are moments when we glimpse our own destructive patterns as well as those of our mate. Yet most couples continue to avoid discussing their issues because they have not created a safe space to do so. Through the power of denial, we minimize the destructiveness of our actions. Seeing these weaknesses in ourselves and our mate but dismissing them has been called the height of codependency and enabling.

We all cope in whatever way we can, in whatever ways we know and have learned. We often slip, unknowingly, into old patterns of behavior, like withdrawing, sarcasm, or angry outbursts. Destructive, reactive patterns, which are often at least partially outside of our awareness, are self-defeating and relationship-defeating.

Crystal Raypole writes in her article titled "What Is an Enabler? 11 Ways to Recognize One" that an enabler describes someone whose behavior allows a loved one to continue self-destructive behavior.[8] I agree that enablers don't act the way they do to intentionally enable bad behavior. Rather, they are often unaware of the impact of their actions, and this is one aspect of codependence.

Enabling doesn't mean you support your loved one's destructive behavior, but excusing it, ignoring it, and even coping with it can be enabling, which does not help the situation. Enabling and codependence are hurtful to ourselves and others.

8. Crystal Raypole, "What Is an Enabler? 11 Ways to Recognize One," *Healthline Media*, June 27, 2019 (www.healthline.com/health/enabler).

While Jack might have framed what he was doing as coping with the increasing tension in his marriage, it didn't really play out that way. He definitely enabled destructive patterns to continue. He watched as Cynthia withdrew. He turned away from her depression when he could have taken a keen and compassionate interest.

Jack wasn't coping effectively. He was withdrawing as well—into his friends, into his alcohol, into his work. He was becoming angrier, hurting more. This was destructive coping.

Cynthia also coped in destructive ways, enabling dysfunction, which only exacerbated problems between the two of them. She stopped confronting Jack's bad behavior, ignoring his excuses for drinking, his growing need to hang out with his buddies, for staying late at work. She focused instead on her children, which offered her pleasure and some relief from her pain.

ESCALATED CONFLICT/ POOR PROBLEM RESOLUTION

The combination of unresolved conflict, disillusionment, detachment, and destructive coping leads to the more serious problem of increasingly escalated conflict and the erosion of a relationship.

Resolving conflict is absolutely essential to having a successful relationship. Problems are inevitable and resolving them is mandatory; otherwise, goodwill evaporates and is replaced by resentment. Couples who cannot resolve conflict inevitably end up with even more conflict, which ultimately leads to marriage failure.

Couples must have the ability to talk about anything, having established tried-and-true methods for facing issues effectively. Anyone who believes they can simply skirt around problems, avoid them, or not face them is in massive denial, and they will definitely pay the price at some point.

In his article "Creative Problem-Solving," Greg Smalley writes:

To a significant degree, the adventure of marriage lies in the challenge of facing difficulties and solving real-life problems together...

Like any vessel on a long voyage, the ship of marriage will almost certainly have to weather some storms. Successful couples realize that this is inevitable...Because they understand this, these couples don't flinch at the prospect of trouble. They don't consider it strange when trials come upon them (1 Peter 4:12). They don't blame one another when misfortunes arise.[9]

This is so true and so critical. Couples who thrive are able to sit down with one another, value each other's point of view, and get on with the task of finding solutions both can appreciate. Couples in the midst of marriage failure cannot resolve problems.

This was certainly the case with Jack and Cynthia. Remember, according to Cynthia, Jack became immediately defensive when she brought any concerns to him. She became weary trying to resolve problems with him and eventually gave up and withdrew.

Although Jack believed he was willing to solve problems, he blamed Cynthia for all of their problems and denied having any part in her issues. His withdrawal, however, was evident by his absence from home, hanging out and drinking with his buddies.

Between them, the fires of resentment grew.

INCREASED RESENTMENT

There are few things more corrosive to a relationship than resentment. The Bible says, *"Get rid of all bitterness, rage and anger, brawling and slander, along with every form of malice"* (Ephesians 4:31).

Why does Scripture take such a strong stance on bitterness and resentment? Why is it so important to eliminate resentment from our lives? Because resentment has been described as the poison pill we take when seeking revenge on another. In other words, when we harbor bitterness and resentment, we are only harming ourselves. We harbor corrosive feelings that will destroy both us and the relationship.

---

9. Greg Smalley, "Creative Problem-Solving," Focus on the Family, January 1, 2014 (www.focusonthefamily.com/marriage/creative-problem-solving).

Resentment and compassion cannot coexist. Neither can resentment and love coexist side by side. When emotional space is consumed with resentment, there is little room for positive feelings and expressions of care and concern.

WHEN EMOTIONAL SPACE IS CONSUMED WITH RESENTMENT, THERE IS LITTLE ROOM FOR POSITIVE FEELINGS AND EXPRESSIONS OF CARE AND CONCERN.

What impact does this have on marriage?

Cynthia's resentment for Jack grew, becoming stronger. Resentment, unfortunately, creates fuel for even more resentment and anger. The more resentment she felt, the more she became obsessed with his drinking, his friends, his work. Can you see their marriage dying?

Jack harbored resentments of his own. The more Cynthia withdrew from him, the more he fantasized about being with someone who cared about him, respected him, and wanted him both emotionally and physically

Jack and Cynthia's mutual resentment fueled the fires of distance, detachment, and destructive coping, propelling their marriage closer to its end. How could it do anything but push them further apart? Both began to seriously consider life apart from the other.

CONSIDERING DIVORCE

When both spouses are consistently miserable with each other, the couple inevitably moves into the next stage of marriage failure: thinking about life apart from one another. Considering divorce is a monumental step. This thinking goes against vows of commitment and plans to spend life together forever.

Considering divorce is both a symptom of relief from distress and simultaneously a source of distress. No one wants a divorce, at least initially. No one wants to give up on a life bound together by memories, good and bad, joys and sorrows, faith, family, and a future together. Yet, this stage of marriage failure is tragically real.

As matters grew worse for Jack and Cynthia, she began having physical symptoms associated with her profound unhappiness. She spent more and more time away from Jack. In many ways, she no longer considered herself married. She began making plans for a life without Jack. She was no longer committed to making it work.

Jack's resentment grew, as did his destructive coping. He spent more time in his basement, watching television, or out with friends. Not wanting to fight, he avoided Cynthia. He convinced himself this was how all married couples related, but deep down, he knew it wasn't true.

An article in *Woman's Day* entitled "Should I Get a Divorce? 17 Signs Your Marriage Might Be Over"[10] cites many of the issues I have written about in this chapter. Some of the signs are:

- Feelings of self-doubt
- Feeling chronically devalued by your mate
- Your partner no longer makes an effort to improve the relationship
- You no longer wish or choose to make the effort
- You no longer support or listen to each other
- Decreased intimacy
- Increased fighting and stonewalling
- Daydreaming about being single

Jack and Cynthia had all of these symptoms. Both were miserable, both felt unsupported, and both knew their marriage was dying.

---

10. Denise Schipani, Lenore Skomal, Nicol Natale, and Corinne Sullivan, "Should I Get a Divorce? 17 Signs Your Marriage Might Be Over," *Woman's Day*, January 4, 2021 (www.womansday.com/relationships/dating-marriage/advice/g2587/signs-your-marriage-might-be-over).

In some ways, Jack was right—a lot of people live miserable existences so he continued to believe that other people didn't have it any better. Justifying his feelings, he did nothing to save or revive his marriage.

It is natural, at this point, to move into the final stage of relationship dissolution: resignation.

RESIGNATION

We've all felt resignation, especially after we've tried everything we know to change things, without success. Maybe we didn't try everything, of course, but *we tried everything we knew to do at the time*. We've exhausted our resources. We've depleted our energies and slipped into resignation partially as a way of protecting ourselves from further discouragement.

Looking back over our decisions can be both productive and a perilous thing to do. It's true that hindsight is 20/20. We learn to make better decisions by making mistakes. But really looking at our mistakes, investigating them, and reflecting on them is often painful.

Jack and Cynthia had already reached the stage of resignation more than a year before Cynthia kicked Jack out and filed for divorce. Cynthia reached the stage of resignation before Jack, but he was not far behind. She was done with living in the shell of a marriage. She was weary of Jack's anger, his withdrawal, and his drinking. She felt intensely lonely.

Jack's response was typical for him: he got angry and frustrated. Although he knew their marriage was over, he was not going to be the one to call it over. He would have continued to hang on had Cynthia not asked for their separation.

Like many other people, they thought of separation as an exclamation point on the end of a sentence. It was a time to say a final goodbye. No more hopes, no more wishes, no more magical thinking. This is the end. Any faint hopes they had of a wonderful ending were gone. Gone. This was truly a time of resignation.

DO NOT RESUSCITATE/DIVORCE

Separating is one thing; divorce is another matter altogether. There is a huge span between choosing to separate, which leaves some room for reconciliation and resuscitation, and filing for divorce, which is so very final.

> **MANY COUPLES SEPARATE FOR YEARS. THEY HAVE NO REAL HOPE FOR RECONCILIATION, BUT NEITHER SPOUSE HAS ENOUGH COURAGE OR CLARITY TO MAKE THE FINAL DECISION.**

Many couples separate for years, living in a no man's land—not married, not divorced. They have no real hope for reconciliation, but neither spouse has enough courage or clarity to make the final decision.

By the time Cynthia told Jack to leave, she was really done with the marriage. She had been planning the separation for a long time. She had given up hope years ago. For her, their separation was only a formality and didn't hold the emotion it did for Jack.

Jack knew Cynthia wanted out, and he realized their marriage was heading for divorce, but he had not yet reached a point of total resignation. Many spouses arrive at this stage at different times, and such was the case for Jack and Cynthia.

The death of a marriage is like the death of a loved one. You have mixed feelings about saying goodbye to your spouse. The relationship, after all, wasn't all bad. There are positive memories interspersed with the negative ones. There are memories that are tainted but still part of one's story, one's history.

Divorce is painful, final, an ending. It's giving up a part of your life and closing the door on it, perhaps like it never existed. It's like burying a dream and shoveling dirt over it.

CLOSING THOUGHTS

It is never easy to see a relationship failing at the time. We're too close to see anything clearly. It is only later, after the fact, that we are able to be reflective and attempt to understand why something happened.

We do know, however, that marriage failure doesn't happen in a moment. It doesn't happen in a climactic event but rather in a long, complicated series of events—patterns of dysfunctional behavior and patterns of failed attempts to keep love and marriage alive.

Marriage failure happens one action at a time, one stage at a time. In the days ahead, with enough reflection, the death of a marriage will be seen as happening gradually but definitely.

Jack and Cynthia were on a downward trajectory early in their marriage. Unable to talk about difficult issues, they didn't resolve their problems and subsequently built a chasm of resentment between them. It's easy to see how self-destructive patterns, combined with a lack of healthy interpersonal strategies, were their downfall.

This is true for many couples I see. In a sense, Jack and Cynthia's marriage was headed for failure early on for all of the reasons discussed in this chapter. When these issues crop up and are not addressed, no one should be surprised when the marriage fails.

Even after years of disappointment and failure, it's hard to face the death of a marriage. It's hard to admit failure is imminent. Perhaps that is why many take so long to reach the decision to end a marriage. Perhaps naively, they think the next time around will magically be better.

What can we learn from any autopsy? We can learn why there was a death. We can learn what caused the death and perhaps learn more about what kinds of mistakes and missteps are fatal. While it is never enjoyable, this stark look at reality can be good for everyone.

How are couples able to find the help they need? What are the barriers to seeking out and receiving help? Acknowledging serious issues and being willing to reach out for help are requirements for any couple seeking lasting and crucial change. But first, we must learn about the barriers that prevent couples from getting the help they need.

PRELUDE:
MAX AND JENNY

"Not another counselor!" Max complained. "How many have we seen already? Six? I am not going to see another one of those goons. I don't trust any of them."

"Max," Jenny replied sharply, "our marriage has never been in worse shape. The counselor is not the goon. You are. You are selfish and self-centered and if you can't see that, well—"

"Look who's talking, Jenny," Max said sarcastically. "Look who's yelling. I'm calm and you're yelling. Every counselor has said you shouldn't be calling names or attacking character, and look who's doing that?"

"Yelling? Why do you think I'm yelling?" Jenny asked. "I'm not an angry, name-calling person. You are resisting counseling again. You always have a reason for not going, and this time we really need it."

"You need it more than I do, so go," Max said. "I'm busy and it's a huge hassle to break away from work for something I don't believe in."

"This isn't too much to ask if you really want to save our marriage," Jenny said. "I want a heart commitment, not you just putting in time. I'm tired of going to a counselor two or three times and all you do is complain. Then we go to another because you think the last counselor was not a good fit for us and we start all over. I am so frustrated. Every book I've read says it is important to be in counseling."

Max laughed. "Jenny, who do you think makes the money from all those books? Who do you think gets something from all the counseling? The authors of all those books and the counselors. We're sure not getting anything from it."

"We might if you would really participate," Jenny said. "You don't listen to any of the advice they give. You always think you know more than they do. Then when they call you on your stuff, you get irritated and won't go back. You're not really there to learn. Can't you see that?"

"They're all speaking psychobabble, Jenny," Max said. "The last guy looked at his watch the entire time and our time was up before we hardly started. *You* even complained about that. We're doing just fine on our own. I don't think we need to make any major changes we can't do on our own. I think you need to stop complaining and give it a rest. Our problems aren't as big as you or any of the counselors we've seen make them out to be."

"You've haven't taken any of the counseling seriously, Max," Jenny said. "Our problems *are* big. You haven't even read one of the books I've bought for us. Counseling could help us if you would go and really listen to what they're saying."

"But they're not saying anything, Jenny," he shouted. "The books don't really say anything. The counselors don't really say anything. My grandma gives better advice. C'mon, you can see that, can't you?"

Max paused and then began again. "We don't need the books, Jenny. Marriage is not rocket science. You act like all we do is fight."

"It seems like we're getting along to you," she said, "because I'm holding so much in. I'm getting more and more resentful and you don't even notice. Can't you see how unhappy I am? Nothing changes. We come home and get back into a routine and I tolerate more before my resentment overflows and we end up in a huge fight. I want to go back to Dr. Jones and I want to follow what he says to do."

"What makes you think that guy has any answers?" Max said. "His marriage is probably no better than ours. I haven't learned a thing from him and we're hundreds of dollars poorer. We've spent enough money on counselors to take a nice vacation, which would help our marriage a whole lot more than the counseling."

"You can't put a price on getting help," Jenny countered. "We need to do whatever we need to do. All those counselors have tried to help us, but it's not the counselors, Max. It's you!"

"Whether it's me or not, I don't want to do it," Max said. "I'm busy and don't have time for this. I will go one more time, but I don't believe in it. It's just money down the drain. No offense, but this all seems stupid to me. One counselor after another, none better than the other. A few handouts, a couple of Scriptures, some *good word for the day*. It's really a joke."

"We're not making progress on our own, Max. Can't you see I'm not convinced about counseling either, but I don't see any other options? Are we doing something wrong?" Jenny asked. "We don't practice what they tell us. Maybe it's not them. We're the common denominator in all these failed efforts. We can't figure this out on our own. I want to keep going. I'm tired and I feel like it's our last hope."

"If you're giving me an ultimatum, I'll go, but I won't like it. I don't really believe in it. This is the last time for me."

RESISTANCE AND BARRIERS TO GETTING HELP

To love at all is to be vulnerable. Love anything, and your heart
will certainly be wrung and possibly be broken.
—C. S. Lewis

Jenny and Max's experience is, unfortunately, extremely common. Most couples share the same experience: try these exercises, read these books, come back in a week or two for a time-limited session, repeat many of the things they've already shared, and then discontinue their counseling after five or six sessions. Most couples become very exasperated with this process, and rightly so. Most couples don't feel like the experience was helpful or that their marriage was in a better place after counseling. These attitudes and experiences create real barriers to seeking help in the future.

Why are couples so resistant to counseling, and what are the specific barriers to seeking help? Jenny and Max's experiences illustrate many of the reasons why seeking counseling is so difficult. Whether we're talking about getting help for our marriage or finding a repairman for our washing machine, finding the right help is often challenging.

I am not comparing marital challenges to washing machine malfunctions but pointing out that finding help for whatever problem we have is often frustrating. Most of us groan at the thought of calling a washing machine repairman, auto mechanic, cell phone company, or marriage counselor.

MARRIAGE IS SUCH A PERSONAL AND PRIVATE MATTER THAT THE VERY PROCESS OF REACHING OUT FOR HELP CAN TRIGGER ANGST.

The very process of reaching out for help triggers angst for most of us. It's often easier to find a mechanic to fix your car than it is to find someone to help with your marriage. Marriage is, after all, a very personal and private matter. Marriage is also a challenging endeavor, as we have learned in the previous chapters.

Marriage is a blending of lives, a blending of different values, different life experiences, different preferences, and different cultural inclinations, which sets the stage for many challenges.

Despite these challenges, we continue to choose marriage over being single. We want to share our life with this other person, and we naively believe it should be easier than it is. But marriage *is* difficult, and most couples need coaching or counseling at some point in their relationship.

In spite of the significant issues, studies show most couples don't access counseling—or if they do, they don't find the experience useful. Not finding the counseling beneficial, and with so many barriers to finding good help, most resist getting help in the future.

Let's understand those barriers and the reasons for resistance to counseling.

DENIAL OF THE PROBLEM

It is human nature to believe we can handle our own problems, especially personal ones. We believe we are capable of handling everyday problems, and marital problems fit into that category. Our head tells us there will be conflicts along our relationship path, but we can handle them as they come up, right?

It is also human nature to resist seeking help. After all, who hasn't resisted calling the doctor, the dentist, the auto mechanic, the contractor, or the handyman? Who hasn't found countless reasons for putting off calling someone to fix the leak under the sink or finding out why the car is making that funny noise, often until it's too late?

Admitting to the severity of marriage problems is more challenging than you might think. It is easy to slip into denial. Minimization of problems, a form of denial, is common. Many feel shame about seeking help for their marriage. After all, what if they discover they are the one doing something *wrong?*

"We're doing just fine on our own. I don't think we need to make any major changes we can't do on our own," Max said. This is a case of severe denial.

And so it goes. Couples may rationalize, justify, and minimize their problems for many reasons, and so they avoid seeking help.

"No one else I know goes to counseling," a man said to me recently. "None of my friends go and I'd be embarrassed if they knew. Nobody talks about going to counseling, or if they do, it typically is something negative."

Many have this same experience. Looking around and thinking you're the only one needing help makes it doubly difficult to reach out for help. It becomes easier to minimize or rationalize your problems.

Imagine looking in the mirror and thinking, "My marriage is in horrible shape, and I'm responsible. I can't make my marriage work." The result of this honesty might lead one to wonder, *What is wrong with me? Others don't need help, but I do.*

Given this uncomfortable scenario, denial kicks in.

There is an acronym about denial that is apropos: Don't Even Notice I Am Lying (to myself). We tell these lies—through minimization, rationalization, and excuse-making—to avoid facing the real issues. We lie to ourselves to protect our egos. We lie to ourselves to avoid feeling shame, regret, and even guilt. We lie to ourselves so we don't have to dig deep, take big risks, and seek help for what seems to be insurmountable problems.

Denial takes many forms and sneaks up on us. That is, after all, what makes it denial. We don't know we're using it. Denial is sometimes minor and sometimes severe. Perhaps you are able to admit that your marriage is in trouble, but you deny the severity of it. Perhaps you acknowledge problems, but deny any real need for change. Perhaps you admit problems, but deny any personal responsibility.

Beneath a façade of normalcy, we may have a faint idea we're in trouble. We may have some inkling that the situation is getting out of control. Yet we desperately want to appear normal and push these thoughts away. Jenny can be seen vacillating in her desire for change, admitting that she tolerates more than she wishes to tolerate, presumably in hopes that things will change for the better.

Most of us have a desperate need to appear normal. We want to fit in. We don't want to think we're worse off than anyone else, and this desire provides the impetus to deny our problems. Denial, then, creates an enormous barrier to seeking counseling.

MAGICAL THINKING

Another aspect of denial that inhibits us from seeking help is *magical thinking*—the belief that *things will automatically get better without any significant changes.* We can all be guilty of magical thinking at times. We admit the problem, at least partially and intellectually, but we believe it will magically take care of itself. Out of sight, out of mind.

Max used magical thinking when he said, "We're doing just fine on our own." Counseling is meant to be a collaborative process, with the couple and the counselor working together as a team. Max thinks, magically, that he has the power to overcome their problems, to figure things out on his own, when their history reveals he is wrong.

Many people have emailed me indicating they hoped their marriage would change, that they would overcome their marital troubles with little help. Invariably, they have discovered that their problems are not resolved. They often seem somewhat surprised by this, but close inspection reveals they've received too little help, usually too late. Or perhaps they found some glimmers of hope and believed those would lead to greater change—but they didn't.

Notice that magical thinking contains an element of gullibility. Note a wife's naivete when she hopes for a breakthrough with her husband if they take a mini-vacation. She believes just a glimpse of hope will lead to a drastic change. Just going away for a few days, having a good time, enjoying nice meals, and experiencing physical intimacy—*this* is supposed to be enough to fix their deep-seated issues?

"Things will get better," we magically believe. Or we rationalize, "Things can't get any worse. Everything will be fine. There are a lot of good things about our relationship; it's not all bad."

> MAGICAL THINKING AND OTHER ASPECTS OF DENIAL INHIBIT COUPLES FROM REALLY SEEKING THE HELP THEY DESPERATELY NEED.

This magical thinking, far from helping, actually makes matters worse. Magical thinking and other aspects of denial inhibit couples from really seeking the help they desperately need. Magical thinking lulls them into believing their situation is better than it really is.

EMOTIONAL LAZINESS

Another significant barrier to getting real help is emotional laziness— not wanting to put in the real work necessary to solve problems.

Remember, within each of us is the notion that it is better to cling to the devil we know rather than risk being with the one we don't. Specifically, we're all inclined to cling to our own situation because we know it. Our circumstances are familiar to us and lead to *emotional laziness*, the tendency to believe our life will be fine, even if we don't exert any effort.

Emotional laziness may take the form of avoidance of difficult situations. It may take the form of believing a mate will do the hard work needed. It may take the form of justifying one's own actions as being enough, when they are anything but that.

Emotional laziness is fueled in part by a desire to maintain the life one has carefully chosen. In some respects, even a troubling situation is familiar. Many cling to their familiar life even if it is painful. It is the life that they *know*, which brings a degree of comfort.

If Jenny is like the countless women I have counseled in similar circumstances, she may wish she had reached this point of crisis sooner. Few reach this point and are glad it took them as long as it did. Most look back with regrets.

But here again, emotional laziness takes a toll. Complacency, comfort, and denial create an emotional space where it becomes easier to settle for the way things are. Many spouses wish, in retrospect, that they had had the emotional strength and energy to create change. They wish they had brought an ultimatum for change to the relationship. But emotional laziness sets in, and couples make accommodations to the life they know.

Emotional laziness stops many people from seeking the help they need. Inertia, a relative of emotional laziness, is another barrier to seeking help.

INERTIA

Another key issue that prevents couples from getting the help they need is inertia—not caring to put in the energy required to change the way things are.

Isaac Newton's First Law of Motion tells us that a body at rest will remain at rest unless an outside force acts on it. Written more than three hundred years ago, these words still have powerful implications.

Notice that Newton proclaims that our body will remain at rest unless an outside force acts on it. Now, applying what we learned about how the frog in the kettle will slowly boil to death without realizing it, there may be no significant force acting on the couple in distress—at least not enough to prompt change. Therefore, unless Max experiences enough anguish, unless he is confronted with a greater negative consequence, he is likely to remain in his troubled situation indefinitely. We shouldn't be surprised by this.

Many couples, including Max and Jenny, complain about their marriage. They may grouse about one another, even *to* each other, but this complaining will likely not be enough to lead to significant intervention or change. They believe, like the frog in the kettle, that the water will never reach a boiling point. Until it gets unbearably hot, or the situation becomes intolerable, inertia prevails.

Max and Jenny's chronic state of unhappiness in their marriage is partially explained by Newton's law of inertia and partly by the notion of emotional laziness. If Max anesthetizes himself with justifications, rationalizations, and magical thinking, we can see why his *body at rest* might remain at rest. We can see why his marriage in trouble might very well remain in trouble.

BLAME-SHIFTING

Another very real barrier to seeking help is blame-shifting—placing the responsibility of our problems onto someone else. Blame-shifting allows us to sit in the bubble of illusion, perhaps even delusion, contentedly thinking *we* are not responsible for the plight we're in. Our problems are because of our mate.

This age-old barrier to seeking help, blame-shifting, is nothing new. We all know about it because we've all seen it, been victimized by it, and possibly wrapped ourselves up in the cocoon of it.

Blame-shifting has been a part of humanity since Adam and Eve.

And he said, "Who told you that you were naked? Have you eaten from the tree that I commanded you not to eat from?" The man said, "The woman you put here with me—she gave me some fruit from the

tree, and I ate it." Then the LORD God said to the woman, "What is
this you have done?" The woman said, "The serpent deceived me, and
I ate." (Genesis 3:11–13)

In this powerful story, we see Adam and Eve frantically avoiding
responsibility. Adam blames Eve, and Eve blames the serpent. I'm surprised the story doesn't have the serpent passing the blame onto someone
or something else.

Insisting, "It's not my problem" is such a common, primitive tactic.
Tragically, this tactic, like all other defenses, protects the blame-shifter
while also keeping that person utterly stuck. After all, if *it's not my problem*,
then there is no need to grow, no need to change, and no need to wrestle
with any issues.

You can certainly see how debilitating such a tactic is, and the profound barrier it is to seeking help. As troubling as this is, however, there are
even more barriers and challenges for us to consider.

DIFFICULTY ACCESSING HELP

Another very real barrier to seeking help has to do with access to help.
Think about this: if a couple is struggling in their marriage and they are
willing to receive help, how are they to find it? Do they simply Google
"marriage help near me"? Visit the online Yellow Pages or review sites like
Yelp?

Seeking marriage help can be a bit like finding a needle in a haystack;
it is challenging, to say the least. The average person has no way of easily
accessing help. Will they ask a friend? This runs the risk of exposing something for which they may feel shame, so this option has limitations.

Consider a couple who are motivated to seek help and have navigated
the arduous path of obtaining a recommendation for a marriage counselor.
What about the issue of credentials? How does the average person know
what kind of credentials are best? If they are able to navigate this issue,
how will they know if the person has specialized training and the requisite
experience to provide marriage counseling? It is very difficult to know if
the professional really has the experience and training to perform marriage

counseling. It is nearly impossible to determine if this professional is really skilled in their craft.

Sadly, when it comes to credentialing, in many states, you can practice marriage counseling by purchasing a business license. How crazy is that? And how vulnerable is the consumer of such services?

Perhaps the couple decides to talk to their pastor, a common gate-keeper to mental health services. While many pastors readily admit that they practice counseling, most do so without any special experience or training. Simply the willingness to provide counseling is enough to allow them to begin to practice it.

Now add another layer of complexity to this already challenging situation. The more credentialed the professional is, the more experience they have, the more expensive they are likely to be. Cost, then, becomes another significant barrier to seeking help.

Finally, let's layer on the issue of time required to attend counseling. Most counselors have limited hours and availability, requiring the person seeking the counseling to fit into the professional's schedule. While it really cannot be any other way, this is a barrier to seeking help.

TALKING TO A STRANGER

Perhaps you've navigated the challenging path to admitting that you need help and even have a recommendation of a professional. What about the issue of sharing your deepest secrets with someone you've never met? This adds yet another layer of complexity to an already delicate situation.

"It's no one else's business!" Max has said.

Is this a valid reason for not seeking help? Of course it is. I've heard this retort a thousand times when asking the question, "Why didn't you seek help?" It is frightening to seek help from someone for the first time. It is uncomfortable to reach out for help in a very vulnerable area of one's life, unsure of whether you will receive compassion and understanding or criticism. As a result, many people remain stuck in their struggles for fear of reaching out for help.

Not knowing who you will be talking to, plus inertia, emotional laziness, and perhaps a dose of blame-shifting all combine to keep a couple stuck and resistant to seeking a counselor.

Social scientists inform us we are only inclined to share with others to the same depth and extent they share with us. We are most comfortable sharing our deepest thoughts and concerns only if the other person reciprocates. Yet this is not the nature of the professional counseling experience.

In her article "How Self-Disclosure Affects Relationships," Kendra Cherry says:

> Building a successful relationship involves a mutual give-and-take between partners. Self-disclosure may be more limited in the early stages of a new relationship, but part of the reason people grow closer is that they become progressively more open to sharing with their partner.[11]

Cherry is referring to friendships and romantic relationships, of course. However, I believe many of these principles apply to all relationships. When seeking professional help, most of us want to know something about the person with whom we're sharing the details of our lives. We want to know this person is trained, experienced, and trustworthy. While the counselor may be a stranger, we want to have a sense that they are genuinely interested in our well-being. This doesn't always happen between counselee and counselor, and it's a legitimate barrier to seeking help.

So, talking to a stranger about very personal matters can be challenging. This places a burden on the counselor to build rapport, create trust, and inspire confidence. If the counselor fails to do this, the therapeutic relationship may be very short-lived.

We have reviewed many reasons why people won't, or don't, get the help they need. Resistance to seeking necessary help is understandable given all the inherent barriers. What about adding another layer of complexity—when the help doesn't help?

---

11. Kendra Cherry, "How Self-Disclosure Affects Relationships," Verywell Mind, November 5, 2020 (www.verywellmind.com/how-does-self-disclosure-influence-relationships-4122387).

WHEN HELP DOESN'T HELP

There are *so many* barriers to getting help. In a way, I cannot blame anyone for not reaching out to a marriage counselor. Given all the obstacles, it's a wonder anyone finds their way to one.

Yet another major barrier to seeking and receiving help is when a couple has experienced help that doesn't really help. The gap between what they hoped for, and what they received, is too great. Left with profound disappointment, many couples simply refuse to try counseling again.

So many couples have said to me, "I have never felt like counseling helped us."

Many women have told me, "I've shared how it seems like my husband is able to manipulate the counselor so that I'm never heard. Shouldn't they be able to see through a man's manipulations? Aren't they supposed to be trained enough to cut through the smoke screens and get to the real issues?"

Many men have said to me, "I'm not as verbal as my wife. I don't stand a chance in counseling. The people we've been to haven't really helped us to change. They gave us some books to read, some exercises to do, but honestly, we could have gotten all of that out of a book."

> **ALL IT TAKES IS ONE BAD EXPERIENCE TO SOUR A COUPLE ON SEEKING HELP IN THE FUTURE.**

All it takes is one bad experience to sour a couple on seeking help in the future. Think about it. Both Jenny and Max felt disappointed in their earlier experiences, which made them hesitant to meet with yet another counselor. If they don't walk in the counselor's door with confidence that this person will help, there will already be resistance to change.

To be fair, *the counselor must prepare the couple for counseling,* and most don't do an effective job of that. The counselor should make it clear how to best utilize counseling, what the couple can expect from the experience, and what they should not expect from it. The counselor must do their part to create a collaborative relationship, teaching couples how to do their best work in between sessions. Most counselors, sadly, don't do this, leaving the couple to flounder with unmet expectations and disappointment.

WHEN HELP IS HURTFUL

Trying to work through unmet expectations and unclear guidance, a couple can leave the counseling office feeling more troubled than when they entered it. How is this possible?

Many couples have shared with me that they have gone to counselors who would ask the same question, week after week: "What do you want to talk about?" Of course, couples want to be asked about their concerns, but they desperately need direction. What they *want* to talk about may actually be the last thing they *should* be talking about.

Many counselors dive right into talking about the latest fight, which sadly may serve only to stir up bad feelings again. The counseling office should not be a place where the couple's last argument is continued.

A counselor trained in marriage counseling knows they must listen to the latest fight with an ear toward the patterns that emerge. They should not simply help to resolve the problem of the day. That process could go on indefinitely. The couple needs to learn new skills so that ultimately, the counselor works themselves out of a job.

Too many couples have shared with me, "We always left in worse shape than when we came. In many cases, counseling made matters worse."

It's no wonder couples quit counseling. It's no wonder they're reluctant to start counseling again. They should expect a counselor to get to the root of the problems, help them see the unhealthy patterns, and then guide them into longer-term resolution.

Sadly, Max and Jenny's experience is common. So many couples go to a counselor only to receive generic feedback, quotes from a book, and a smattering of guidance offered in clichés. This is not helpful and leaves a troubled couple even more disillusioned than they were before they entered counseling.

WHEN HELP IS HARMFUL

We've covered many layers of barriers to getting the marriage help that's needed. One more especially troubling barrier is having experiences that not only don't help but are actually harmful. This troubling scenario is a common occurrence.

In Dr. Scott Bea's article titled "Can Therapy Hurt You—and How Can You Tell It's Not Working," he writes:

> If you feel misjudged, unduly criticized or humiliated in therapy— which are some of the things that prompt people to seek help in the first place—that's not good, and you'll need to find another thera- pist…Sometimes therapy isn't hurtful, but it also isn't helpful. For example, if you leave therapy feeling better for a few days but are not developing new attitudes, skills or strategies for change, that's nice support, but it's not psychotherapy. It won't help you find more effective and flexible strategies to face the problems of living.[12]

Counseling should help. Period. Counseling, as Dr. Bea suggests, should guide you into cultivating more skills, strategies, and new ways of viewing your situation. You should receive expert guidance and not simply a listening ear. You should be able to look back and see where you are rela- tionally ahead of where you started. You should feel the progress; both partners should be able to emphatically say, "This is helping." If not, you should question what you're doing.

It's not easy, however, to give up on counseling. That may not make sense in light of what I've been saying about barriers. However, both can be true—there are many barriers and much resistance to getting help, but once the decision has been made to get help, it may not be easy to admit it's not working.

---

12. Dr. Scott Bea, "Can Therapy Hurt You—and How Can You Tell It's Not Working," Cleveland Clinic, October 18, 2019 (health.clevelandclinic.org/can-therapy-hurt-you-and-how-can-you-tell-its-not-working).

Think about it. If you've decided to get help, you've overcome some major hurdles. If you don't feel helped, it is typical to believe that perhaps you're doing something wrong, rather than assuming there is something wrong with what the counselor is doing. It is a bold step indeed to confront a counselor and suggest that what they're doing is not only not helpful but is actually hurtful. Most will simply disappear, perhaps never to return to counseling.

A GROWING RESISTANCE

All of these issues are cumulative, creating layers of barriers that add up to either a positive experience or a negative one. In too many instances, the cumulative impact for the couple seeking help is negative, with increasingly greater barriers to seeking and receiving the help they desperately need. This, of course, points to even greater chances of a marriage failure.

All of the issues listed in this chapter create real barriers to getting help. We've covered a lot of information—so much that even my head is spinning. It is no wonder couples find it hard to get the help they need. It might help to review the barriers we've covered:

+ *Denial of the Problem*—falsely believing there really is no problem. Denying a problem works to push an issue out of our minds, but just like the frog in the kettle that's slowly getting hotter, the problem gets worse, and the results are even more disastrous.

+ *Magical Thinking*—falsely believing the problems in the marriage will magically disappear. No greater work is needed. No further actions need to be taken.

+ *Emotional Laziness*—falsely believing no greater energy is needed to find a solution to marital problems. The couple assumes that either what they're doing is enough or that the energy they are expending should remedy the problem.

+ *Inertia*—falsely believing one doesn't need to address issues of inertia. Here there is a natural, inherent problem: a body at rest remains at rest unless an outside force acts on it.

+ *Blame-Shifting*—falsely believing the responsibility for the problem lies with someone else, so no further action is required to create change.

+ *Difficulty Accessing Help*—falsely believing accessing help should be easier. Here one believes it is simply *too difficult* to find good help and subsequently gives up.

+ *Talking to a Stranger*—falsely believing talking to someone new about personal matters should not be so difficult and subsequently deciding not to do it.

+ *Help Not Helping*—falsely believing professional help should always help, and if it is not helpful, one is entitled to give up.

+ *Help That Hurts*—falsely believing help should never be hurtful and if it is, one is entitled to give up.

+ *Help That Is Harmful*—there are circumstances where getting help has actually been harmful.

Can you see the overwhelming challenges to getting marital help? There are so many barriers, many couples choose to simply go it alone, read some books, or settle for the way things are. This leaves couples who are struggling with even more trouble and without hope.

A LOSS AND LACK OF HOPE

Think about a situation in your life where you've lost hope. Hope is the belief that what is wanted can be obtained. Couples in trouble hope to have a wonderful, life-enhancing relationship. Many are sorely disappointed and discouraged, lacking any kind of vision for change. This is the final barrier to getting the help they need.

We've reviewed the many barriers to receiving help at a time when hope is diminished. Max and Jenny feel weary, discouraged, and hopeless. They aren't really convinced anyone can help them. This attitude does not create an impetus for seeking help.

It's said that nothing breeds success like success. The corollary to this would be, "Nothing creates a loss of hope like lost hope"—the point being that hopelessness builds upon itself. Discouragement gains fuel with increasing disappointments.

We all know this to be true, but it is even more poignant and discouraging for the couple who have experienced barrier upon barrier to receiving good help. They are already struggling, having experienced loss day in and day out, so the layers of barriers to getting help are all the more daunting.

> ## COUPLES IN DISTRESS ARE DESPERATE FOR HOPE AND ENCOURAGEMENT. IF HOPE IS NOT BUILT INTO THEIR COUNSELING, THE COUPLE MAY RETREAT IN DESPAIR.

Couples in distress are understandably anxious for a bit of hope. They are, in fact, *desperate* for hope and encouragement. If a skilled counselor doesn't recognize this and find ways to immediately build hope into their counseling, the couple may retreat in despair.

Perhaps this helps to explain why couples in significant distress succumb to the many barriers to receiving help—in other words, they have lost the goodwill and motivation to overcome those barriers and haven't received the hope and encouragement they desperately need.

Disappointment breeds disappointment. Inertia certainly breeds inertia. Hopelessness breeds hopelessness. Inaction breeds inaction.

CLOSING THOUGHTS

Let's revisit Max and Jenny's situation. They've been to five or six different counselors and feel no better for it. In fact, matters may now be worse because they have many negative experiences to overcome with a new counselor.

Now, several counselors later, with very little hope, they appear to have managed to muster an ounce of hope, but it is small and fleeting. With such little hope, their experience must now be positive, encouraging, effective, and helpful, or they are at great risk of giving up.

Again, who can blame them? They would obviously not be the first to decide it simply isn't worth the effort. They would, in fact, be justified in not expending more energy on a process that has not proven fruitful for them.

The failure for Max and Jenny is, at this juncture, not on their shoulders alone. Counselors have failed them, pastors have failed them, families have failed them. They have failed each other. But, at this moment, there is a spark of hope as they seek help yet again.

Let's now consider what couples like Max and Jenny can expect as they seek help.

PRELUDE: JAN AND BEN

"You're the one who needs help," Jan said impatiently. "I've been going to counseling for years, and you've never been willing to work on yourself."

"That's not true," Ben countered. "Not true at all. I went to that men's prayer group for a couple of years, and I've gone with you to counseling three or four different times."

"A prayer group is not counseling, Ben," Jan said. "Seeing our pastor a few times does not mean you've been open or willing to change. You just went to check off the box. Every time we've gone to a professional, you haven't really participated and you sure haven't changed."

Ben grew angrier. "Look, I hate when you act so high and mighty. I hate that just because you've read every marriage self-help book, you think I should do the same. I don't have to do everything the way you think it should be done. You don't have as much figured out as you think you do."

"Unbelievable, Ben," Jan said. "I work on myself because I know I need to change. I expect you to do the same. I've been to counseling and have asked you to come with me. You never go. I've suggested we find a counselor we both agree on, and you always make excuses."

"We've tried counselors, Jan," Ben said. "They don't help me. Don't you get that? They can't make us get along. That's up to us. Besides, I'm not going in to talk with some woman you've already shared your version of all the issues with who already has an opinion about me. You don't really expect me to do that, do you? And, seeing the pastor has been helpful to me. I resent your telling me who I can and can't see."

"Sitting with Pastor Dan and praying about our marriage doesn't change you, and I need you to change," Jan said. "I need you to see someone who helps you change."

"You are so incredibly controlling," Ben said. "You want to dictate who I am going to see for counseling. That's crazy. I should be able to talk to whoever I want to talk to and you should have nothing to say about that."

"I want to have some say over who you see, Ben," Jan said. "I want to see you change, and everything you've done so far has made zero change. Nothing. So, you can see who you want, but if nothing changes, then what?"

"Then maybe it's not all me, Jan," Ben said. "Maybe it's time for you to look in the mirror too. Think about that."

"I have spent hours looking in the mirror," Jan said. "I've gone to a professional counselor for years. I've always been the one to get us into counseling. I've been the one to push for help in so many ways. I'm exhausted. I'm asking you to join me now."

"You're not going to bully me into this, Jan. I don't think I need professional help," Ben said. "You're not going to change my mind about that."

READINESS FOR MARRIAGE COUNSELING AND SEEKING HELP

I'm a very strong believer in listening and learning from others.
—Ruth Bader Ginsburg

Are Ben and Jan ready for marriage counseling? To be prepared to receive help, both spouses must come with an open mind, as we talked about in the last chapter. Both must be ready to hear what the other is saying and seek to understand the truth in what they're saying. Both must be willing to let their spouse point out what they see without becoming defensive.

Counseling is not a forum for having a power struggle. It's also not a place to attempt to coerce your mate into changing. Rather, it is a place of safety where both individuals share their concerns and both come ready to make some concessions to their mate. It's a place to learn more about each other and grow together.

Ben clearly isn't ready for couples counseling. He has his mind made up that he is not responsible for any of the marital problems. Jan seems to be much more open-minded. This combination does not lend itself to challenging marriage counseling.

What happens if one partner doesn't agree with the other? That is actually expected. If they agreed on everything, they wouldn't need counseling. Still, there must be some degree of openness to hear the things that are hard to hear. They must agree that seeking help has some potential value for both of them.

Many of us have been where Jan and Ben are today, locked in a desperate struggle to make sense out of what is happening but using tools that are ineffective.

We've all wondered if there really is such thing as a person who can coach us into a better place. Can't we manage our problems alone? Most of us desperately want to feel adequate and self-reliant when it comes to our marriage. Do we really need a counselor to get us where we want to go? Or, is good counseling possibly a combination of our efforts and the direction of a good counselor?

Jan and Ben are like many other couples. They may believe their marital toolbox is full, but instead of a box filled with effective tools, theirs is filled with rusty, broken tools. Unfortunately, their tools consist of blaming the other, coercing the other, and calling in others who might side with them to bolster their point of view. They believe they are right while their mate is wrong.

Could you hear Jan and Ben blaming each other? You might not have noticed because this is the way many couples attempt to solve problems. Could you hear the *he said/she said* arguments? Jan and Ben created a battlefield, each entrenched in their own position, not really listening to the other and certainly not validating the other's point of view.

Furthermore, the tension in the room rises each time one criticizes the other. You might not have noticed that either, because many couples fail to notice emotional escalation until it's too late. The tension increases with each criticism, possibly outside of their awareness. Neither seems to have the wherewithal to shift into a collaborative position. Neither seems willing to give any ground.

Unfortunately, this is a recipe for disaster. Their process of blaming each other, unless redirected by the most skilled clinician, is certain to escalate and lead to even greater conflict. Even if a counselor has managed to redirect them, if the couple refuses to give ground and listen to each other, their process is doomed to fail. They will end up in one of the places discussed in the last chapter, refusing to really participate in counseling or failing to make good use of the process.

Marriage counseling is a collaborative process, meaning both spouses must be prepared to yield ground if their efforts are to succeed. They must let each other know that they really care about their spouse's perspective and what they need. This is the glue that holds a couple together.

Let's explore additional requirements for successful counseling.

COUNSELING EXPECTATIONS

Any journey taken with another person requires an agreement about expectations. If you don't know where you want to go, you can't possibly get there. So, you must have some idea where you are going and what you want to achieve. Without this agreement, there will be a tug-of-war, as we saw with Jan and Ben.

> A COUPLE MUST DO THE HARD WORK OF AGREEING ON WHAT CHANGES THEY WANT TO MAKE AND WHAT THEY WANT FROM EACH OTHER.

This initial step, often taken before even seeing a counselor, is critical. A couple must do the hard work of agreeing on what changes they want to make and what they want from each other. To be fair, not all couples know these things before they begin counseling, but if they don't, discovering these answers must be one of the first tasks.

For as important as it is to agree upon expectations, many couples enter into counseling very unclear about what they hope will happen. Many couples believe it is simply a forum for airing grievances, with the mistaken notion that the counselor will side with one of them and make the other see the error of their ways. They use counseling in an attempt to manipulate the other.

This is not a reasonable expectation of counseling.

Some individuals seeking counseling are aware of this error, but most are not. For example, it is not likely that Jan would admit she seeks counseling to change Ben, though she has suggested as much. This seems to be her intent. Neither would Ben admit he hopes the counselor will side with him.

What is likely to happen if both enter counseling with the intention of changing the other? Unless the problem really is clearly the responsibility of one person—which is rarely the case—the outcome for counseling stands a good chance of being compromised, or worse, ending in failure.

Even in the case of emotional abuse and domestic violence, where one person's egregious actions have solidified the need for counseling, the other partner will likely need to make some changes too—different changes, to be sure, but changes nonetheless.

When one partner has serious character issues, the other still has work to do in setting boundaries, expressing feelings in a healthy way, and finding their own path of recovery. Both have work to do, albeit different work.

Again, when a couple enter counseling without an agreed-upon outcome, and lean heavily on finding fault in the other, it is a recipe for disaster.

BEING PSYCHOLOGICALLY MINDED

Having the right attitude and approach to counseling is mandatory. The right attitude means having some understanding and agreement that most problems are cocreated. Even when they are not, counseling requires both people to make changes for healing to occur. Having this attitude is no small feat; it requires what has been called being psychologically minded, having insight, and being teachable.

You might think that everyone is *teachable* and that going to a *relationship coach* implies that you want to be coached. Psychological mindedness—having an awareness and insight into one's contribution to relational problems and being open to learning more about one's contribution to the marital issues—is not a given.

Yet from the outset, a couple must acknowledge that they are both part of the problem and will be an integral part of the solution. This insight, this psychological mindedness, is vital if progress is to be made.

Can such thinking be taught? Can a person learn how to be coached and counseled? Yes, though it takes some level of openness, willingness, and humility. These are qualities a good counselor will highlight and cultivate as the counseling process begins.

Some people do well in counseling right off the bat. Why is that? Because some people are prepared for couples counseling, perhaps even having an understanding of the counseling process, while others simply are not. Some people are ready to own their part of a problem, while others actually resist this process. Being open, ready, and willing to learn is a key ingredient for a successful counseling experience.

Most wrongly believe they are open-minded, ready to learn, and ready to hear from others. This simply is not the case. Being psychologically minded is a sophisticated character trait, often developed with hard work. It means being able and willing to be reflective, to receive critical feedback without undue defensiveness. It means being curious about how you move through the world, how you face adversity, and how you relate to others.

Being psychologically minded means being very self-aware. It means being able to stand outside yourself and monitor your actions as well as your thinking. It means being able to think about your thinking, being open to new ideas, and being curious about how you are functioning.

Most of us know someone with the opposite mindset. You know the type: rigid in their thinking, unaware of the negative impact they're having on the world, stuck in right/wrong and good/bad thinking, self-centered. They believe they are always right and their mate is wrong.

These people are often insufferable, difficult to be around and, not surprisingly, very difficult to work with in counseling. In fact, these people often refuse to attend counseling because they rarely see themselves as having any problems. The problems in their world are all *out there*, not in themselves.

While M. Scott Peck didn't use the phrase "psychologically minded" in his famous book *The Road Less Traveled*,[13] he must have been thinking of this type of person when he spoke of their opposite: individuals with character disorders who thought any problems were because of others, not themselves. Lacking insight, defensive, and dismissive of others, these people certainly feel distress, but they blame it on the actions of others. They don't readily enter into counseling. If they *do* go for counseling, it is most often at the urging, even a threat of some kind, by someone significant in their life.

Being psychologically minded certainly enhances the counseling process, and practicing the mindset of getting outside of yourself should be a prerequisite for couples counseling. There are also other factors that indicate whether or not someone is willing to seek out and benefit from couples counseling.

BEING READY FOR COUPLES COUNSELING

Having appropriate and clear expectations of couples counseling is vital. Being psychologically minded, having the capacity for insight, and being teachable are critical factors. However, there are even more requirements to be ready for couples counseling.

Certainly, not every couple seeking counseling is really ready to benefit from the process. I've learned this lesson the hard way. More than once, I've sat with a couple and watched and listened to them fight, feeling helpless to stop the exchange of insults. More than once, I've actually spoken up and told the couple I would no longer be a witness to their verbal struggle.

---

13. M. Scott Peck, *The Road Less Traveled: A New Psychology of Love, Traditional Values and Spiritual Growth* (New York: Touchstone, 1978).

Benefiting from couples counseling, as I've said, is not a given. Helping a couple know exactly what to expect, and what they can do to make the most of the counseling process, makes them more likely to succeed and maximize the benefits it provides. Here are some additional requirements for a couple to be ready for, and actually receive, help:

1. Being Clear and Open About Their Desire to Heal Their Marriage

Both spouses should look at one another and voice their commitment to healing and saving their marriage. You might think this goes without saying, but it doesn't. Being crystal clear about this intention is reassuring and provides great impetus to do the forthcoming hard work.

Something powerful occurs when a couple looks at each other, especially in the midst of distress, and voices a commitment to working through issues. Perhaps threats have been made to separate or end the marriage. These threats may be real and need to be discussed. Still, voicing a desire and intention to work through issues is powerful.

Heartfelt listening, with the desire to understand and empathize, is a key component of couples counseling, changing the listener as well as the one speaking.

2. Being Ready and Willing to Listen to One Another

The couple must be willing to not only listen to one another but also seek to understand and empathize with the other's experience.

The late theologian Paul Tillich said, "In order to know what is just in a person-to-person encounter, love listens." This doesn't mean simply hearing what the other is saying. Rather, it means listening in a deep and understanding way, truly *getting* this other person, as someone unique and distinct from us.

This, again, is so fundamental, it might seem to go without saying. Of course, we expect our mate to show a genuine interest when we share our truths and our experiences. We expect to be able to share our thoughts and have our mate not interrupt and, in fact, care deeply about us.

Many show up for counseling so wounded, so filled with hurt and sadness, they literally do not have the emotional space to hear their mate. In extreme circumstances, one might even say to the other, "I don't care what you think. You've hurt me so badly, I don't want to hear what you think."

This is, of course, a nonstarter. Counseling cannot continue if one person will not or cannot express genuine interest in what their spouse has to say. The willingness to listen to your mate's experience is a primary prerequisite for effective counseling.

Notice, in Jan and Ben's interactions, how both interrupt the other, talking over each other. Neither seems genuinely interested in what the other thinks. Their process of communication, the way they talk to each other, is as much a problem as the specific issues they bring to counseling. Their process has become their central problem.

3. Being Willing to Validate Your Mate's Experience

Not only must you be willing to listen to your mate and learn about their experience, showing genuine concern, but you must also be willing to validate their experience.

Validation has been described as the ability to show that we affirm and recognize the reality of what the other person is expressing, even if we disagree—in other words, conveying that the way they see the world is understandable and makes sense, especially given who they are and their life experiences.

To validate another person, you could say, "Anyone might feel what you're feeling in your situation," or perhaps, "What you're feeling makes sense. I can see why you feel that way."

Validation takes effort. It takes getting out of our head and into the head of our mate. It takes setting aside our own experience to truly grasp how our mate views the world.

Notice how Jan and Ben oppose each other's experiences, failing to validate their mate's point of view. Jan discounts Ben's efforts at emotional growth and cites her work as the only legitimate way to bring about change. Both not only fail to validate their mate's experience, but they are dismissive and even derisive about their mate's perceptions of the world.

4. Being Willing and Able to Empathize with Each Other

Empathy has been described as the glue that holds a relationship together. Brené Brown, a leader in the field of empathy, shares four important steps needed for empathic connection that contribute to a positive counseling experience:

+ Perspective taking, or putting yourself in someone else's shoes

+ Staying out of judgment and listening

+ Recognizing emotion in the other that you may have felt before

+ Communicating that you can recognize that emotion

Make no mistake, empathy takes real effort. Think about it. To put yourself in another's shoes means straining—yes, straining—to see the world through another's eyes. Their experience is not your experience, but you must strive to imagine their experience. Their thoughts are not your thoughts, yet you must strive to understand how they think, what they feel, and how their experience is vital and meaningful to them.

It is shortsighted to say to another, "I can't understand your experience." What this means, more often than not, is that the listener is emotionally lazy and unwilling to expend the energy to *be in another's shoes*.

It means hearing without really listening.

One particularly lazy response is to sit only with sympathy for another. We feel sorry for them rather than taking the time and energy to fully imagine what is happening within them.

Brown asserts "Empathy fuels connection while sympathy drives disconnection. Empathy is I'm feeling with you. Sympathy, I'm feeling for you."[14]

Empathy and sympathy are often talked about as if they are the same thing, but they are very different. Empathy connects us to another while sympathy often actually creates distance. Empathy is a learned skill that brings people together. It is a primary tool in couples counseling.

---

14. Dr. Brené Brown, "The Power of Vulnerability," RSA talk, August 15, 2013 (www.youtube.com/watch?v=sXSjc-pbXk4).

Notice with Jan and Ben that they show absolutely no empathy for the other. Neither shows any effort to fully understand the other's experience. It seems as if they are oblivious to the fact that their mate sees the world through different eyes. They give no indication that they understand that their spouse's experience is different from their own.

5. Being Ready to Collaborate on Problems, Seeking Solutions That Benefit Both Spouses

The concept of collaboration may be the most necessary prerequisite for successful counseling. However, it is no small feat. It means suspending your sense of what is *right* in favor of working effectively with this other, unique person.

I love the word *collaboration*. It might be my favorite word in the dictionary. And why not? One definition of collaboration is *win/win*. You win, I win. Who can argue with that? We agree to seek out solutions to our problems by ensuring no one walks away the loser.

Without collaboration, in a very real sense, if one mate wins, the other loses. Losing is likely to breed resentment rather than foster a joyful, harmonious spirit between them. This is a powerful concept to bear in mind.

For a couple to admit they've been engaged in a power struggle is often quite challenging. Most see themselves as collaborative. They are reluctant to admit they are in a power struggle, seeking to *win* over the other. Yet this often is precisely the case.

While few admit wanting to win, many secretly harbor this perspective. Few acknowledge this intention, but it exists nonetheless. Many harbor an attitude where the most powerful, dominant, vocal person *wins*, and by definition, the other loses. Is it any wonder that this process breeds resentment?

Many couples believe they are simply trying to *make a point* and function under the illusion such actions are innocuous. They are not. Some believe they have *greater insight*, a *more practical perspective*, or perhaps *greater wisdom* than others. Fueled by a sense of self-righteousness, many push their agenda and deny wrongdoing. This is typically nonsense. The person referencing the higher authority of greater experience, wisdom, or practicality wants to win, pure and simple.

A good counselor sees this dynamic at play and calls it out. A person willing to be coached admits this underlying attitude and is open and receptive to change.

AS IT PERTAINS TO COUNSELING, COLLABORATION MEANS ENTERING INTO THE PROCESS BEING WILLING TO LISTEN, LEARN, VALIDATE, AND EMPATHIZE WITH THE OTHER PERSON.

As it pertains to counseling, collaboration means entering into the process being willing to listen, learn, validate, and empathize with the other person. It means setting aside your personal agenda. It means being intent on seeking *win/win solutions*, so both parties walk away from the interaction feeling good.

Not once did Jan or Ben make any mention of the other's needs. Neither seemed to take the other's desires into consideration. There is no mention, on either part, of seeking solutions satisfying both parties. Again, this is a recipe for disaster.

6. Being Willing to Put Feelings Into Words and Share Them

The couple must be willing to put into words what they are feeling and be able to share specifically what they need from their mate.

Sharing feelings is our most vulnerable way of communicating. This is generally an accepted aspect of healthy human relations, though certainly not without its challenges. Sharing everyday information, facts, and opinions about life is the least vulnerable form of communication, while sharing feelings is our deepest point of connection.

Why is sharing feelings so critical to being ready for couples counseling? Because if you cannot share your feelings, you are typically not ready to communicate vulnerably, and sharing vulnerably is the way emotional connection takes place. Sharing feelings is the beginning of solving emotional problems.

Sharing feelings is a rather tricky business. Many believe they are sharing feelings when, in fact, they are sharing opinions. A few examples:

+ "I feel like you don't love me." This is not a feeling at all but rather an opinion, a criticism.

+ "I feel like you are too critical." Again, this is not a feeling but an opinion, a criticism.

+ "I feel like you are a wonderful person." Again, this is not a feeling but an opinion, and a rather nice one at that.

So, you see, many mistake opinions for feelings. Learning the art of sharing feelings, speaking vulnerably, is a relevant aspect of being ready for couples counseling. When someone knows what they feel, what often naturally follows is knowing what they need. If one is able to communicate this, real progress can be made in couples counseling.

Sharing feelings and speaking vulnerably are critical in order for two spouses to truly know each other. To know what one thinks is no doubt important, but to know what one feels and subsequently, what one needs, is imperative for a healthy relationship.

7. Being Able to Envision What They Need and Share It With Their Mate

Knowing what you feel and need is one thing. Being able to share these with your mate is an entirely different matter. Can you see how these skills layer one upon the other?

Spouses who are truly able to access and receive marriage counseling are able to know their feelings as well as their needs and share these effectively with their mate. You might be surprised at just how challenging this can be, especially if you are not versed in practicing this intricate skill.

Think about it. We all know when we're missing something in a relationship. Our feelings scream either satisfaction or dissatisfaction. Our bodies record our reactions. If we are tuned in at all to our bodily sensations, we know happiness or unhappiness. Being able to articulate the problem is yet another skill.

Being tuned into our feelings and listening to them, knowing what might be missing for us, is tricky business. This requires a keen sensitivity to our feelings. Knowing what is missing in our relationship is definitely a step in the right direction; however, being able to articulate it effectively creates a real opportunity for change.

Notice that I use the word *effectively*. Many of us know how to complain, but complaining doesn't effectively share a need. Many know how to get angry and make accusations. However, accusations do not cause a mate to want to come to assist. In fact, anger and accusations typically push another away. So, learning how to share a need in such a way as to be effectively heard is quite a skill—and a necessary one for marriage counseling.

Another critical component of good marriage counseling, and effective relating, is making sure you are doing your own work and not that of your mate.

8. Both Must Do Only Their Own Work, Not Try to Force the Work of the Other

We cannot, of course, speak for another person. While we can and should imagine what they might feel, we should never tell them what they're feeling or thinking. We must never drift into their space, telling them what they should or should not do.

When we believe we know why our mate is doing what they're doing, or worse, when we claim to have the answers to their problems, we are out of our lane and into theirs. They alone are responsible for their life. Venturing into our mate's work is a serious violation, but it's one that many make. Additionally, taking the focus off ourselves and our personal work and focusing on our mate is not only ineffective, but adds to relationship conflict.

Finally, we can certainly ask for changes from our mate, but we dare not try to force or coerce them to change. No one changes against their will. In fact, when forced, most will be uncooperative and resist our efforts.

9. Being Willing to Let Go of Self-Protection and Share Vulnerably

Learning to share feelings and needs vulnerably requires letting go of self-protection. This is quite a tall order but a necessary one for effective marriage counseling.

Letting go of self-protection is not as easy as it sounds. We learn to protect ourselves naturally. Everyone has developed ways—some known and others only in our subconscious—to guard against being further hurt. It is in retreating that one learns to guard against harm. It is by going on the offensive, *bullying* others, that we attempt to get them to back down emotionally. It is by being *lawyer-like*, arguing one's point of view, that we vainly try to maintain emotional control.

Each of these tactics may temporarily protect us, but simultaneously harm ourselves and our mate. These methods of protection also create distance and disconnection; they cannot function well with the goals of counseling. Rather, counseling calls for vulnerability, sharing feelings, and seeking to connect with another in an intimate way.

> COUNSELING CALLS FOR VULNERABILITY, SHARING FEELINGS, AND SEEKING TO CONNECT WITH ANOTHER IN AN INTIMATE WAY.

Someone once described intimacy as "into-me-see," leading to emotional transparency. Into-me-see is letting others see who we are, what we're thinking, and what we feel on any given topic. Self-protection cannot coexist with into-me-see—emotional intimacy. Every couple must choose whether or not they want true connection or self-protection. They are mutually exclusive concepts and actions.

10. Being Willing to Talk About Their Wounds and Accept Healing

A couple must be willing to articulate how and where they have been wounded and be open to receive healing. Marriage is, in a sense, a dangerous place because it's a place where you are the most vulnerable. We choose to live with another, allowing them to see our strengths as well as our weaknesses. Living with another, in all varieties of circumstances, allows others to see behind our social façade.

It is here, beneath the façade, where you can also be wounded. Your mate knows just what to say to wound you if that is their intention. They are capable of wounding you by bringing harsh attention to your weaknesses.

Wounding can take place in many ways, and again, an effective counseling process exposes this troubling pattern of behavior. Wounding can take the form of harsh and derogatory words, expletives said to hurt, and actions taken to deliberately hurt or taken accidentally that still hurt. Violations of trust, faithfulness, and honesty can be particularly damaging.

Marriage counseling, done well, exposes wounds and patterns of wounding. In exposing these wounds and patterns of wounding, an excellent counselor brings the opportunity for healing. The counselor shows how the wounding party may be the best person to speak healing words and bring healing actions to bear on the troubling situation. The counseling experience becomes a place of healing.

Being ready for couples counseling means being willing to be vulnerable and open to talk about where and how we've been wounded. It also means being open to listening to, and empathizing with, your mate in ways they have been wounded.

11. Being Willing to Allow the Counselor and Mate Speak into Their Life

Critical feedback never feels good. It takes a thick skin to accept and even embrace it. Counseling is a change process, always involving critical feedback.

Being ready for marriage counseling means embracing and even leaning into this criticism, knowing the result is emotional growth. It is here, in the safety of a counselor's office, that you let down your self-protection and critically examine your life and your marriage.

If a couple has the good fortune of finding a skilled counselor, they must allow this specialist to speak into their lives. Self-protection, again, doesn't really serve anyone. It serves to keep one safe, but also keeps one very stuck. Thus, it is wise to really listen to what the counselor, *and their mate*, has to say.

Reminding yourself that your spouse has your best interests and that of your marriage at heart can help you receive critical feedback. They aren't sharing information to hurt you. When this is kept in mind, the sting of criticism is lessened.

In addition to trusting your mate, you must also let go of doubts and trust the intentions of the counselor.

12. Being Willing to Identify Destructive Patterns and Eliminate Them

Both the couple and the counselor must work together to identify their destructive patterns, seeking together to eliminate them. The counseling process will be as effective as the three persons are able to function as a team. With a common goal—to identify strengths and weaknesses in a marriage and develop skills to function more effectively—the three people must work cooperatively. Anything less will inhibit the effectiveness of the counseling process.

Healing old wounds is much easier if one's current functioning is healthier. You must rely on your counselor to lead the way. The couple must allow the counselor to illuminate problems and help bring healthy resolution to past issues. The counselor must be encouraged to teach new skills to move a couple forward.

> **THE COUPLE MUST ALLOW THE COUNSELOR TO ILLUMINATE PROBLEMS, BRING HEALTHY RESOLUTION TO PAST ISSUES, AND TEACH NEW SKILLS TO MOVE THE COUPLE FORWARD.**

The best way to create this partnership is to cultivate a constructive, cooperative relationship, with clearly stated, solution-focused goals. Having clearly defined goals that are measurable will help the team move forward. Any behaviors that disrupt forward progress must be identified, named, and confronted. Taking responsibility for them as well as determining a path for change will create an effective counseling team.

WHEN ONE IS READY...AND ONE IS NOT

What should happen if one partner is *more ready* for counseling than the other? Must both partners be equally ready for counseling when it begins? This rarely, if ever, happens.

We have identified what it takes to make the most of the counseling process. It is rare for a couple to enter counseling with agreed-upon goals and motivations. Typically, one wants change more than the other. Typically, one is more motivated for change than the other. The wise counselor notes these differences and talks about them, collaboratively seeking a solution both spouses can embrace.

In the case of Ben and Jan, they are unfortunately too far apart in their thinking to make good use of counseling. Ben will predictably sabotage the counseling process unless Jan and the counselor are able to win him over, helping him see the value of the counseling.

So, there cannot be too great a disparity between what the two partners expect from counseling. If one is ready and willing to go to weekly counseling, perhaps even participating in intense, multi-hour counseling, while the other is willing to only attend once per month, there is too great a disparity for the counselor to make much progress.

This can be an incredibly challenging issue. Some professionals would say that unless both partners are fully committed to the counseling process, it cannot work. I don't believe matters are that diffinitive. I believe that frequently, one partner has a stronger investment in change than the other, and this disparity alone should not be reason to reject counseling.

The key issue is the *degree* of the disparity. This disparity must be discussed and resolved, with expectations clarified and resolved.

CLOSING THOUGHTS

It may be challenging to think that so much responsibility for counseling success lies on the counselee being an active learner. It may also be challenging to think the counselee must learn how to be an effective learner. Many think walking through the door of the counselor's office is enough to warrant progress. That, sadly, is not the case.

Just as in any new endeavor, be it learning to speak a foreign language, picking up a musical instrument, or entering a new profession, the person must be ready and willing to learn and be prepared to dedicate time and effort into the learning process. Gaining as much as possible from counseling is much the same. Attitudes toward learning make all the difference in the world.

Being a good student or learner means taking an active interest in the process. Remember, one must be open to criticism, be psychologically minded, and insightful.

The teacher, of course, must be willing and able to teach, or, as in the case here, the counselor must be skilled and ready to engage the counselee in effective ways.

What happens if the counselor is resistant, outdated, and unskilled in marriage counseling? We'll explore these issues next.

PRELUDE:
GARRETT AND KARA

"You have to go to counseling, Kara," Garrett said.

"No, Garrett, I don't," Kara said. "We've tried that and each time, you go for a few sessions and then quit. I'm done."

"You can't be done," Garrett said. "What about our girls? What about our marriage? Give it one more try."

"I don't want to, Garrett," Kara said. "The girls are fine. You only want to go to counseling now because I don't. You've fought me on this for two years. What's up with you now?"

"Let's go and see if this time works. I know I haven't been easy to live with. I get that. Just one session and we'll can go from there. Please."

"One session, Garrett," Kara said, "and only if I feel good about it. Then we'll go from there."

Garrett asked around for names and came up with a marriage counselor. They scheduled an appointment.

"What brings you two to counseling?" the counselor asked at their first session.

"Our marriage is in serious trouble," Garrett said. "Kara's ready to leave and I don't want that. We need help in sorting things out. I've been difficult to live with. I know Kara has a lot more to say, so I'll let her talk."

Kara rolled her eyes. "Difficult to live with doesn't even begin to describe what I've been through," Kara said. "But before I get into that, I've got some questions. I'd like to know more about you and your credentials. How long have you been in practice?"

"Several years," the counselor replied.

Kara looked carefully at the certificates on the wall.

"Have you had special training in marriage counseling?" Kara asked.

"I have a full counseling schedule," the counselor replied. "I see single people, married people, kids and families. I have kind of a general practice. I don't know what you mean by special training." She paused, then added, "I like working with couples, sitting with them and listening to their concerns."

"Look, I don't mean any disrespect," Kara said. "But do you have any special training in marriage counseling? Do you know much about difficult men? Because I'm married to one. I'm ready to leave him. I don't have time to just talk over everything I've been through. I'm not sure about any of this. I'm so close to being done."

The counselor shifted in her chair. "I've worked with different men and women with all kinds of problems. I am licensed to counsel. I have a bachelor's degree in communications and a master's degree in counseling. Do you have some specific concerns?"

Kara looked over at Garrett.

"What about difficult, angry men?" Kara asked again. "We've been to counselors before and they don't seem to get it. They don't understand what I've been through."

"Get what?" the counselor asked.

"They don't get how challenging a selfish, angry man can be," Kara said.

"We want to be certain you can help us," Garrett said. "We've been to other counselors with mixed results. We really need positive results this time."

"The results haven't been mixed, Garrett," Kara said. "There hasn't been any change." She turned to the counselor. "Can you confront him and will there be real change?"

"I do what I do," the counselor began, "but the major work is up to you. I make suggestions, and it's up to you to put the suggestions into practice. Why don't we begin and see what happens? I can certainly listen to both of you and we can all decide together if it's working. How does that sound?"

"I've got a few more questions," Kara said, growing more exasperated. "Do you have a particular way you work with couples? Do you have a method or system that you use? The last counselor had been trained in a particular method. I forget what it was, but there was a certain format to the counseling. There was homework and some reading we had to do. There were some skills we had to practice. What do you do?"

"I listen to a couple each session and then together we agree on how we will proceed. I think couples will find their own solutions. Most of the couples I've worked with have liked working with me."

Kara and Garrett looked at each other again, feeling doubtful about proceeding. They had made it this far and paid for the session; it seemed too late to turn back now. They shared more of their story while the counselor listened.

On the drive home, Kara was quiet, looking out the car window.

"What are you thinking?" Garrett asked Kara.

"That seemed like another waste of time to me," Kara said. "She didn't have any plan. She doesn't have any special training. She just let us talk. She thinks people can find their own solutions? What does that mean anyway? I didn't get anything out of it."

"Yeah, a total waste of time," Garrett agreed, obviously frustrated. "I'm not sure she even listened. She didn't point anything out we didn't already know. She didn't challenge us in any way. She didn't give us any homework. We're just supposed to come back next week and she'll know more then?"

"She didn't even hide looking at her watch," Kara said. "That was a big sign that she wasn't really present with us."

"So, what do we do now?" Garrett asked. "I counted on this. Please say you won't quit now. Don't you think we owe her another chance?"

"Garrett, our marriage is in shambles," Kara said. "If I'm going to continue, it won't be with mediocre help. I need to feel confident any counselor we see works with us and challenges us. I need to know the counselor understands what it's like to live with an angry man. If I'm going to be *in*, we have to find the best help we can. My vote is to move on."

"How do we know the next one will be any better?" Garrett asked.

"Well, I'm not going to keep seeing this one," Kara repeated. "I don't have any confidence in her."

COMPLACENT, OUTDATED, AND POORLY TRAINED COUNSELORS

For the things we have to learn before we can do them,
we learn by doing them.
—Aristotle

Marriage is tough business. Counseling a couple in crisis is an equally tough business, both for the couple and for the counselor. Both the counselor and the clients are incredibly challenged, in different ways.

To many, counseling appears to be an easy job. It's not. It's certainly more difficult than I imagined it would be during my early days of training. I could never have imagined at the beginning of my career that clients and their conflicts could be so challenging. Nor could I have known at that time I would need to learn far more than I was taught in school to be a strong and effective counselor.

I entered the field of counseling believing, as many young counselors do, that all I had to do was listen well, and all would go smoothly in the counseling office. I followed the advice of famous psychologist Carl Rogers, who said all we had to do was form a compassionate, caring relationship where the client felt heard. If the counselor listened well, there would be counseling success.

This was not good advice. Counseling is far more complex than that.

While listening is certainly foundational to successful counseling, good counseling requires far more than listening. Counselors who enter the field with the notion that good listening equals good counseling will discover a deeper reality very quickly. They will learn, or should learn, that it takes extensive training and experience, in addition to a listening ear and a compassionate heart, to be a good counselor.

A SUCCESSFUL COUNSELOR NEEDS MUCH MORE THAN A HUGE HEART AND COMPASSION FOR EMOTIONALLY HURTING PEOPLE.

I've already said that many couples enter marriage with a great amount of naivete. The same is true for counselors entering the field of counseling. Too many counselors begin their careers believing that a huge heart and compassion for emotionally hurting people are enough to be successful in the field of counseling.

They are wrong.

Most counselors quickly learn the hard way that effective counseling requires more than a college degree and some on-the-job training. Most learn the hard way, through clients dropping out of counseling, that they are doing something wrong.

RED FLAGS

Counseling is not simply a soft science, where the clinician listens well, offers some advice, and invites the client to show up the following week. That can be done, to be sure, but that is not a recipe for good counseling.

It is not unusual for many clients to see multiple counselors throughout a marriage. When a counselor does not retain a client, they are often quick to place fault on the client, rather than questioning whether they may be responsible for the client not returning.

"They are resistant to counseling," one counselor told me recently, referring to a couple who came for two sessions and did not return. "They're just shopping for a counselor who echoes what they want to hear."

Is that really what is happening, or is there more to the picture? Is it possible that something is terribly wrong with the counseling system? Is it possible that rather than the client being at fault, much responsibility lies with the counseling profession?

Standing back and reflecting on my extensive training and years of experience, I'm alarmed by the fact that in reality, I've had very little oversight. With so much responsibility, seeing couples in crisis daily in my practice, I've had very little supervision or case consultation with other professionals.

These factors—lack of supervision, lack of case consultation, and lack of training—are all serious red flags and are true for many counselors.

Consider these truths: many counselors are busy. Clients can come and go, but the counselor's schedule remains full. As long as they're busy, it might not even occur to a counselor that *they* may be the reason clients are not returning. With a full schedule, why would they consider changing anything?

There are far too few gatekeepers when it comes to counseling. With too little experience and too little supervision, combined with too little specialized training, many counselors are left to counsel the way they've always done it. Nothing new, nothing changing.

It is time for both clients and counselors to reconsider the profession of counseling, recognizing some of the red flags I've mentioned.

There are some serious problems. These problems would not be acceptable practices in nearly any other professional field, and should not be in the field of counseling. This results in a large group of counselors who likely began counseling with a few basic tools and an earnest intent to help people in crisis. They now face the challenges of counseling troubled couples and find themselves in over their heads with the skills they have, and no one suggesting that they acquire additional training for situations beyond the textbook.

COMPLACENCE

Complacency can become a problem in any profession. It's a natural occurrence. Counselors, unfortunately, begin with excitement and enthusiasm and, after gaining some degree of proficiency, often become lax, even complacent. Yet, with so much on the line, with people who look to counselors for urgent guidance, complacence should not be an option.

How did I come to the conclusion that many counselors are complacent? I've been counseling for over forty years and must say it is the rare counselor who exudes confidence, interest, and energy in their profession. When I consult with colleagues, I often find a surprising lack of enthusiasm. They seem content to do things the way they've always done them, lacking innovation, not updating their skills or attempting to discover new, more effective strategies.

Many counselors are satisfied with their status quo. They have busy schedules. They know that for every client who drops out because of dissatisfaction, another will call for an appointment. There is absolutely no external motivation for change; frequently, there is very little internal motivation either.

These statements are not meant to paint a bleak picture, but rather to challenge those in the counseling profession to look inward at themselves and consider change. In addition, I challenge the consumers of counseling services to expect more.

COMPLACENCE REINFORCED BY CONSUMERS

Is it realistic to expect you, the consumer, to demand more from counseling? I'm not entirely sure. How can clients even know they are receiving mediocre services? The markers for good counseling versus mediocre counseling are not clear. Given this lack of clarity, it is easy for the consumer to settle for mediocrity.

Think about this: there is no real way to measure whether the client is receiving the services for which they are paying other than satisfaction. And this is nearly impossible to measure. Either you're satisfied with the service or you're not. And, if you're not, why not?

Can you see the problem?

Since the counselor's clients have no real way of measuring the outcome of what they're paying for, and no real standard against which they can measure what they're receiving, it stands to reason that most clients can only offer dissatisfaction in one way—with their feet. They do not return. Frequently, couples who are dissatisfied with a counselor do just that.

> **WHEN A DISSATISFIED CLIENT SIMPLY DROPS OUT OF COUNSELING, OFFERING LITTLE OR NO FEEDBACK, THE COUNSELOR IS NOT MOTIVATED TO CHANGE OR IMPROVE THEIR SERVICES.**

The client then, unwittingly, reinforces complacence on the part of the counselor. When the client simply drops out of counseling, offering little or no feedback and no clear critique, the counselor simply moves on to the next client, in all likelihood unmotivated to change or improve their services.

FINDING GOOD HELP

The most common way clients comment on the quality of the counselor's skills is by not returning—a very inefficient way of rating a counselor's skills and capabilities.

Knowing how to find a good counselor, or even knowing what constitutes a good counselor, however, is a huge problem. How is anyone supposed to know what to look for in a counselor? Having no accurate way to measure the effectiveness of a counselor, it is no wonder clients settle for mediocrity.

Garrett was faced with a real dilemma. Should he press Kara to go back to the counselor they both found ineffective? Should he look again for another counselor—and if so, how will he find a good one? They sought out a professional, with certificates and credentials to counsel, assuming they would get helpful professional guidance. They left feeling disappointed.

There are very few ways to discover who provides good counseling and who is complacent, outdated, and poorly trained. Scrutinizing certificates on the wall will give you next to no useful information on whether your counselor knows how to provide complex marriage counseling.

There is no real clearinghouse of those ready to assist clients like Garrett and Kara, helping them find good help. Will they simply look on the Internet and take their chances? Probably. Might they ask around, perhaps getting a recommendation from their pastor or family friend? Yes. But again, how reliable is this?

Finding a trained marriage counselor is radically different from finding a reliable mechanic, plumber, or physician. Like many professions, counseling does have apprenticeships and on-the-job training, yet something is missing: information. Since seeking counseling is such a private, personal matter, most are not inclined to *ask around*. They either give up or quietly seek a counselor based on scanty information and run a real risk of being disappointed.

LACK OF INFORMATION

Seeking a good counselor is daunting. People don't know what they're looking for and thus don't know how to make informed choices. Thus, without critical information, many couples make decisions based on a counselor's degrees, which give painfully little helpful information. Reading a counselor's biography on their website reveals their interests, their degrees, and…that's about it.

So how is the average couple to determine if this clinician is truly skilled in their area of expertise? We live in an age of information. We expect information and pride ourselves on being informed consumers, taking the time to learn about the services we're seeking. This is often impossible when it comes to marriage counseling because the information we want isn't there. We want reassurance, even a guarantee, that someone will care about us and provide expert counsel.

Without information, and a lot of it, many of us are reluctant to move forward. Going to counseling is a huge step, and most of us are afraid to take it without the confidence that our action will yield positive results. We all need reassurance that our personal lives will be kept private, that we will be treated respectfully, and most importantly, that this step of faith will work.

Lacking information, the average individual isn't sure how to look for a good counselor, let alone know what they can even expect from counseling. Armed with knowledge about what they can expect would go far to alleviate anxiety in this process. What are some ways to measure success in the counseling process?

CLARIFYING EXPECTATIONS

Garrett and Kara expected answers from their counselor. They expected active interest, hope, encouragement, and clear direction. They were disappointed when they left her office. As it turned out, they voted with their feet—they did not go back.

Was Kara being too demanding when she asked the counselor about her experience and her training in marriage counseling? Certainly not. It is not too much to ask anyone professing to be a marriage counselor be trained, experienced, and skilled at performing marriage counseling. After all, a marriage is in trouble, and two people are begging for help.

Garrett and Kara's need was legitimate. Kara was exhausted and ready to leave her marriage. She was desperate for the counselor to understand the complexities of living with an angry, selfish man. She needed someone who could lead them to make real change.

What exactly did Garrett and Kara expect, and was their expectation realistic? Like most couples seeking counseling, they aren't completely able to articulate their expectations, other than wanting and needing help. They are not sure what to look for in a good counselor. What they *do* know is that what they're doing isn't working, and they need someone willing to take the lead and help them discover what is wrong so they can fix it.

When we look deeper, we find most people have common expectations, although they are not often easily or clearly articulated.

1. Couples Want a Qualified Marriage Counselor Who Offers Clear, Compelling Instruction

While being listened to feels good, and we all want to be completely heard, those seeking counseling want much more. They want, need, and expect *expert* advice. They want clear direction and reasons for giving that direction.

> **MOST COUPLES WANT A COUNSELOR WHO GIVES THEM EXPERT ADVICE, NOT SOMEONE WHO TELLS THEM TO SEEK THEIR OWN REMEDIES.**

Think about your experience with a physician. We typically consult with someone who has extensive training for the physical problems we have. We want to see someone who exudes confidence, is able to clearly articulate the issues, and offers clear direction to remedy the problems.

We do not want to consult with someone unsure of themselves. We don't want to be told to seek our own remedies. We want direction—compelling, clear, and powerful direction.

Not only do couples want wise instruction, they want a confident counselor who is able to convey to the couple that they have the skills to lead them out of the chaos they are currently experiencing and into the calm connection they need.

2. Couples Want a Qualified Marriage Counselor Who Takes an Active Interest in Them

Couples want to work with a marriage specialist who makes them feel like they are the only ones on their mind. They want to feel special and want to sense this counselor will go to great lengths to help them save their marriage.

How do we measure an *active interest?* It is measured by enthusiasm, curiosity, and confidence that the counselor is providing *exactly* what the couple is seeking. It is an alignment of expectations and reassurance for the couple that the counselor is listening. If expectations cannot be met, the counselor makes that clear as well.

Too many marriage counselors are rigidly attached to the *tradition* of counseling. Most counselors work nine to five, Monday through Friday, and are inaccessible at other times to couples who are struggling. This is understandable, but marriage issues don't always fit into a schedule. Crises happen, and the client has a right to expect some availability when in serious trouble.

3. Couples Want a Qualified Marriage Counselor to Offer Keen Insight Tailored to Their Specific Situation

Marriage counseling must be uniquely tailored to the couple. For as much as we might want to think everyone is alike, it's not true. Every couple is quite unique. The talented marriage counselor, trained and armed with experience, must bring their expertise to the couple and offer insight into their specific situation.

Too many counselors fit the couple into their way of working, rather than the other way around. Couples have a right to expect a counselor to work with them according to their singular needs and experiences.

Too many counselors offer generic, cookie-cutter solutions, giving the same general advice and prescribing the same reading materials for every couple. They offer the same handouts, the same advice, the same counsel. They duplicate the same questions and suggestions for everyone—and the couple feels this complacency. Couples recognize this lack of keen insight and walk away discouraged.

4. Couples Want a Qualified Marriage Counselor Who Is Willing to Work Intensively

While the counseling profession has functioned on the fifty-minute hour forever, this format rarely works for marriage counseling. Couples want a counselor who is willing to put in extra time with them when necessary. While couples are typically understanding of the counselor's time restrictions, they want and expect occasional exceptions and become discouraged otherwise. They want allowances made for the crisis phone call, the clarifying email, and the session that went poorly.

Fifty minutes flies by when discussing complex issues. Couples feel unnecessarily frustrated when the counselor tries to pack challenging counseling into fifty minutes. Couples want to know more time can be made available if necessary.

Many counselors fail to anticipate a couple becoming discouraged, overwhelmed, and frustrated. This again points to the lack of training, experience, and sensitivity on the part of the counselor. When a counselor's schedule is packed, with little wiggle room, crises are not effectively met. The result is a couple who does not feel connected or even attached to their counselor.

5. Couples Want a Qualified Marriage Counselor Who Works In-Depth

Stressed for time and following their tradition of the fifty-minute hour, counselors too often offer superficial, limited counsel. Couples correctly sense when a counselor refuses to explore the depth and complexity of issues brought to them. Again, the couple often leaves feeling profoundly discouraged.

Couples are tired of superficial instruction. While brief, time-limited counseling can be effective for some challenges, this process doesn't work well with complex marriage issues. Couples want to work with a well-trained clinician who takes a keen interest in them and their problems, who is willing to spend the time and energy to go deep, uncovering dysfunctional patterns of behavior and assisting them with meaningful, lasting change.

INADEQUATE TRAINING

Why are these expectations not met? What is the real problem? Unfortunately, most counselors are not specifically trained in the art of marriage counseling. Counselors typically have a smattering of training, enabling them to become excellent generalists but ineffective specialists.

This is a huge issue and one not addressed by the counseling profession. No one is required to gain specialized training in order to do specialized work. For example, a counselor does not need a special certificate to work with abused children, angry adolescents, adults with depression or anxiety, or couples in distress.

This is a problem.

Marriage counselors are, as a general rule, in over their heads. Training in counseling individuals for specific issues at any stage of life does not translate into the ability to work with couples.

So many counselors, with limited training, education, supervision, and experience *feel* qualified to do marriage counseling when, in fact, they are sorely lacking in these areas.

MANY MARRIAGE COUNSELORS ARE
IN OVER THEIR HEADS. TRAINING
IN COUNSELING INDIVIDUALS
FOR SPECIFIC ISSUES DOES NOT
TRANSLATE INTO THE ABILITY TO
WORK WITH COUPLES.

AN OUTDATED WAY OF DOING THINGS

The field of counseling has historically been treated as an art rather than a science. In many areas, counselors have been allowed to counsel because they felt drawn to the field of counseling, doing so with limited credentials, if any at all.

Consider pastoral counseling for one. Here, the minister, simply by being ordained and armed with a desire to help, but with little to no counseling training, can have a full counseling practice. The pastor no doubt cares and wants to help, and is sought after to offer a listening ear, but may not have the skills necessary to really help the parishioner. Just because you have an interest in listening to people and helping them solve problems doesn't mean you can actually perform complex counseling.

Why, given the inherent problems, isn't this system of counseling changing? Why isn't more training, supervision, and experience expected of the marriage counselor?

PRACTICING BEYOND COMPETENCE

Everyone resists change. We all get used to doing things the way we've always done them. There's nothing new or unique about this. Counselors, like other professionals, have established ways of doing things, and those practices get handed down from professional to professional.

When counselors fail to obtain the training and experience needed to effectively do what they say they are skilled at doing, they are often practicing beyond their scope of abilities. This is not appropriate; clients are shortchanged and even harmed in the process.

Too often, a counselor accepts clients with troubled marriages, only to find themselves unable to do the work effectively. They may sense they are in over their heads, but either refuse to admit it or do not know how to change the way they are doing things. They may be practicing beyond their competence.

Garrett and Kara's counselor, while clearly friendly, was likely untrained to effectively counsel couples needing far more than a listening ear. Her credentials and training are questionable for doing the work she says she is prepared to do. Is she really capable of handling the challenge of counseling couples in serious distress? Should she be confronted and asked to update her skills?

Working with couples in distress is hard, hard work. A counselor with generalized training and generalized skills cannot possibly do this work effectively.

Anyone seeking counseling has a right to expect that the professional they're seeing is prepared, ready to sit with them, and able to offer expert assistance. This requires specialized training in working with couples in crisis, as we discussed earlier. Anything less borders on practicing beyond their scope of training and expertise.

FAILING TO FORM A STRATEGIC ALLIANCE

Clients are typically only willing to show up week after week if the counselor remembers their homework assignments, offers clear direction, and helps the client formulate the next week's tasks. Clients expect a counselor to know more than they do and speak boldly and encouragingly into their lives, guiding them from conflict to compassionate connection.

Too many counselors have completely failed to form a strategic and powerful alliance with their client. Amazingly, they don't know they have failed to form this alliance. The counselor often believes the client is happy and will return the next week. They're wrong.

Unbeknownst to them, an alliance has not been formed, and the client looks for ways to end the counseling. With mixed feelings, because the client is still in incredible distress, they slip away.

CLIENTS EXPECT A COUNSELOR TO SPEAK BOLDLY AND ENCOURAGINGLY INTO THEIR LIVES, GUIDING THEM FROM CONFLICT TO COMPASSIONATE CONNECTION.

David Burns, a seasoned professional psychologist and author of the book *Feeling Good*, was one of the first to recommend that counselors check in with their clients at the end of each session to ensure alignment of goals. This method of constant feedback, where the counselor is informed by the consumer, helps to ensure the counselor and client are working together effectively to reach the client's goals.

Sadly, most counselors do not practice this feedback loop. Most are oblivious to clients dropping out of counseling, unaware of the dissatisfaction many have with their counseling process. Counseling could be, when all is said and done, a powerful, strategic alliance, where counselor and counselee agree together on a game plan for their problems. The counselor/client relationship could be an incredibly important alliance, no less so than that of doctor/patient, but again, this alliance is often not happening.

Most counselors fail to grasp the severity and urgency of this strategic alliance. They fail to grasp the importance of mutual trust and respect. They fail to understand what is needed in the urgency of the situation. They fail to discern what will bring health to this troubled marriage.

Garrett and Kara went to counseling feeling hopeless and discouraged. They did not know how to articulate what they needed or how to ascertain if this counselor would be effective in helping them. They left with all the problems they had when they arrived at the counselor's office, feeling even more discouraged.

Will Garrett and Kara return to this counselor, and if so, will they persist in sharing their doubts? This is not likely. Will the counselor sense the broken alliance and make necessary adjustments? This is also unlikely. Garrett and Kara, if they are like most other couples, will drop out of counseling.

CLIENTS DROP OUT

Clients like Garrett and Kara give feedback to the resistant, uncaring, and untrained counselor, though seldom in writing or a verbal dismissal. Most dissatisfied clients never say a word; rather, they just drop out. They disappear, never to be heard from again.

Think about it. Garrett and Kara felt a sense of dissatisfaction. They knew they did not receive any real help, but were unsure of what to do next.

Could their counselor have sensed their dissatisfaction? Certainly. At least she had the opportunity to read their cues. They wondered aloud about her credentials and asked about her experience in marriage counseling, particularly in working with "difficult men." When she told them, "I think couples will find their own solutions," Kara and Garrett immediately realized that this counselor would not be able to help them. Her apparent lack of connection left them with feelings of doubt, distrust, discouragement, and puzzlement. Would they go back again? Probably not. Like many couples feeling no bond between themselves and the counselor, they will simply disappear. They don't typically complain. They just drop out. This makes it easy for the counselor to *victim blame*, believing the client is the problem, not them.

This is simply not true. More often than not, a client disappears because they are not getting the help they need. The fault lies largely with the counselor.

CLOSING THOUGHTS

Counseling is a challenging process for both client and counselor. Both parties need to be tough, willing to dig in and do the emotional work. Clients have a right to expect this from their counselor.

Counseling requires cutting-edge preparation and, more than anything, it requires honesty. Candor. The counselor must constantly assess whether the process is working. Failure to do so leads to missed opportunities. Worse, it harms the discouraged client.

Too many counselors are complacent in their approach to their profession. Too many fail to obtain the further training that marriage counseling demands. Counselors are given too much freedom to practice the way they choose and settle for mediocrity, leaving clients like Garrett and Kara to suffer. They are not met with the professional respect and fervor they deserve.

Every client has the right to expect interested, trained, in-depth, tailored treatment, but counselors and the counseling system have failed clients through the lack of industry-wide certifications.

What specifically are the qualities of a good counselor? What are the markers of good counseling? We will explore these questions next.

PRELUDE:
GARRETT AND KARA FIND
A GOOD COUNSELOR

"**K**ara, I know you said just one more time and I take full responsibility for picking her out," Garrett said after their disappointing start with a new counselor. "But please, Kara, can we take what we've learned from this crummy experience and work together to find a counselor who can help us work on our marriage?"

"I told you only one more time, but you agreeing with me about that last experience and offering to work together means a lot to me. So yes," Kara said, "I'll work with you to make a list of what does not work, and then put together a list of what we think we are looking for in a marriage counselor."

"Thank you," Garrett said. "I'm not sure what we're looking for, but I think we'll know it when we experience it."

"I know I want someone who is genuinely interested in us, who really cares about helping us save our marriage," Kara sighed. "I'm close to out of energy."

"Right, no cookie-cutter solutions," Garrett said. "I know I need direction. I am nervous about someone digging in to find out what we're doing that's making our marriage so miserable. But I get it. I need to be open to that."

"I agree," Kara said. "I'm glad you're taking this seriously."

"So, let's talk more about what we're looking for," Garrett said. "I don't want to make the same mistakes again. Let's brainstorm some ideas."

Kara began. "I sure don't want someone who is only looking to fill their schedule, that's for sure. And I want someone genuinely interested in us. I'd like to find someone who is passionate about saving marriages."

"It's got to be someone who has done a lot of marriage counseling," Garrett continued. "It can't be someone fresh out of school. I don't want a counselor who does a little bit of this and a little bit of that. Don't you think we need someone who specializes in marriage counseling?"

"That's a good question," Kara said. "I thought all counselors saw all different kinds of problems. In some of the ads I've been reading, the counselors say they treat kids, adolescents, adults and couples. They list all kinds of problems."

"I don't want that," Garrett said emphatically. "That's the problem we had last time. She said she saw kids and adults, people with depression and couples with problems. I want someone who is really focused, specializing with couples. I want to look for that."

"Okay, so what else?" Kara asked. "How do we know if anyone is any good at couples counseling?"

"I don't think we can know for sure," Garrett said, "but I saw one person listed who belonged to an association of marriage counselors. I think we look for someone with special training and affiliations in marriage counseling."

"Sounds good," Kara said. "I'd also like someone who really listens to us. I want someone who will ask questions. I want someone who remembers what we tell them and gives us specialized help. We've got some really bad habits, Garrett, and I want someone who will address our specific issues."

"Agreed," Garrett said. "Plus, I think you and I said we want someone who will teach us new skills, give us stuff to work on between the sessions. We have a habit of doing fine for a while and then things fall apart. They need to understand that about us. We want someone who tailors the counseling to our needs. Right?"

"Yes," Kara said. "One more thing. I want to like the person and feel like they like us. It's important that we like each other. I know it's a lot, but I need someone who genuinely cares, is compassionate and challenges us to grow."

"That's a tall order," Garrett said. "Let's go online and look at different websites and bios. I believe we can do a better job now of finding someone who will work for us."

"Right," Kara said. "Maybe the counselor who offers a pre-counseling session to see if we're all a good fit. I've heard some counselors do that. What do you think?"

"Perfect," Garrett said. "Tonight after dinner, we go shopping for a person who will help us. Thank you again for giving us a chance."

7

QUALITIES OF A GOOD COUNSELOR

What embitters the world is not excess of criticism,
but an absence of self-criticism.
—G. K. Chesterton

With so much on the line, Garrett and Kara cannot afford to make a mistake when choosing their next counselor. However, how are they supposed to find a qualified marriage counselor? How can they know if a counselor is *good* or *bad* without attending a few sessions?

They have one standout thing going for them: experience. They have experienced bad counseling and have agreed together on some of the qualities they're looking for in the next counselor.

They agree that their next counselor should be someone:

- Having counseling training and credentials
- With a specialty in marriage counseling
- With a lot of marriage counseling experience

- ✦ Genuinely interested in them
- ✦ Dedicated to helping them save their marriage
- ✦ Showing compassion and developing rapport
- ✦ Willing to give clear direction
- ✦ With keen insights and skilled at assessing their marriage problems
- ✦ Who challenges them to grow
- ✦ Who is likable and who likes them

Armed with an understanding of why the last counselor failed, and having a list of qualities they want to see in their next counselor, Garrett and Kara decided to try once more, this time better prepared.

They compiled a list of red flags after their last bad counseling experience, which taught them how to better search for a qualified counselor. They knew it would take a combination of specialized training, education, and experience in marriage counseling to get the help they desperately needed.

In this chapter, we will explore ways that couples like Kara and Garrett can find a counselor who can really help. They made a list of what they want in a counselor, so let's see if we can work through their list to identify someone with those qualities and the training needed to be an excellent marriage counselor.

TRAINING AND EDUCATION

Finding a good marriage counselor to fit Kara and Garrett's criteria, who will be capable of helping them heal their marriage, is no easy task. You cannot determine a counselor's level of skill by reviewing their website.

In today's world, most counselors have a website and typically share pertinent information about themselves, their experience, and their mission. This is a great place to start. After all, what do we all need in order to make informed decisions? Information!

Most counselors' websites will highlight their training and education. Many will cite their experience and even add a bit of personal information to help you get to know the kind of person you would be working with if you decided to hire them.

The first thing to look for with any professional is their level of training. Many counselors enter the counseling profession because they care about people. While this is a laudable motivation for helping others, much more is needed. Caring must be applied on top of a foundation of training.

Reviewing a counselor's website will give some fundamental information, such as where they earned their degrees, which ones they hold, credentials, and professional affiliations. Counselors enter the field from many differing perspectives and avenues, and it is important that you understand these differences.

Some enter counseling from a background of life coaching. While such training can be beneficial, it is not typically considered a profession leading to a specialty in marriage counseling.

Some enter the field of counseling with a pastoral counseling degree, often with a background in ministry. Again, while many have found pastoral counselors helpful, typically this is not considered a degree or background offering a specialty in marriage counseling.

Finally, many entering the field of counseling have degrees in counseling and psychology, some with master's degrees and others having obtained their doctorate in counseling and psychology. These are often considered to be degrees leading to a specialty in marriage counseling.

As with any other professional field, typically, the more advanced degrees the person holds, the better, though this is not always true. Having at least a master's degree or a doctorate in counseling is recommended.

EXTENSIVE TRAINING IN MARRIAGE COUNSELING

Even achieving a master's or doctorate in counseling doesn't ensure that someone is a specialist in marriage counseling. Many if not most counselors with these degrees are generalists and might advertise themselves as such, meaning they see people with a variety of issues. Their lack of clarity and specificity regarding their scope of practice, and lack of specialization, can be confusing to the consumer.

A MARRIAGE COUNSELOR SHOULD HAVE SIGNIFICANT CREDENTIALS AND EDUCATION AS WELL AS SPECIALIZED TRAINING AND SUPERVISED EXPERIENCE.

Marriage counseling is a complex endeavor, requiring the counselor to have significant credentials and education as well as specialized training and supervised experience. Learning whether a counselor has received significant education, training, and supervised experience requires asking the right questions—not always the easiest thing to do.

Consider some of the questions that must be answered to determine if a counselor has had the requisite education, specialized training, and supervised experience:

- What is their education and was it specifically in counseling?
- What specialized training have they had in marriage counseling?
- Do they consider themselves to be a specialist in marriage counseling?
- What is their model for marriage counseling?
- Have they had supervised training and experience in marriage counseling?
- How much experience have they had in marriage counseling and what do they consider to be their success rate?

These are some of the questions I would ask before retaining a couples counselor. These are questions the client *should* ask their prospective counselor. A good counselor welcomes questions from clients who have put thought into their search for someone who can help them.

A counselor with significant experience in marriage counseling will be comfortable in answering these questions. These are basic questions for the seasoned counselor.

Considering the answers given by the counselor will help the couple whittle down the list of prospective counselors to find one who specializes in marriage counseling. While many counselors claim to work with a variety of people and problems, not many emphasize working specifically with marriage problems.

By way of example, consider the field of medicine. While a primary care physician is well-trained to perform a variety of tasks, they admit to not being a specialist and will therefore refer a more acute or complex problem to one. Again, there is nothing at all wrong with being a generalist, but people must be cognizant of the limitations.

Like doctors, counselors are often trained as generalists, with strong skills to help many people. Then there are those who have found they are gifted in a specialized area and seek additional training to learn the unique skills required in that field of expertise.

INTEREST

If complacency is the downfall of the poor counselor, active and even excited interest is the hallmark of the good counselor. The good marriage counselor is genuinely interested in their clients.

Interest, of course, is not something that is measurable. Instead, genuine interest is something you feel, something you sense. How is this done? You can gauge interest by the questions asked, the comments made, and the feeling that the counselor is present with you.

The good counselor shows a keen interest by remembering the homework they gave you the week before. They show interest by remembering details of what you've told them, feelings you've shared, and concerns you perhaps didn't have time to address but which they noted to bring up at another time.

The good counselor will say things like, "I remember we didn't have time last week to address the issue of…" and will bring up the concern that was voiced. "I wonder where you're at with that issue now and whether you'd like to talk about it today."

> ## A GOOD COUNSELOR REMEMBERS DETAILS OF CONVERSATIONS, FEELINGS THAT THE COUPLE HAS SHARED, AND CONCERNS THAT WERE VOICED IN PAST SESSIONS.

This kind of focus and attention broadcasts real interest and concern for you. With all the people a counselor is working with each week, to remember specific details of each client shows dedication to you.

The good counselor is keenly interested in the story unfolding before them. Like an intricate mosaic, the good counselor listens to the broken pieces of the story and begins to see how the pieces fit together. They form a cohesive story from the fragments shared by the clients, and this process creates a level of hope.

The good counselor does not rush this process, however, because jumping to conclusions is actually the mark of a lazy counselor. Counseling involves a certain degree of patience to be able to *see* what is unfolding before them. With enough patience, patterns emerge. From the emerging patterns, the counselor, like the good physician, knows how to intervene.

Still, the good counselor remains flexible, open to seeing things in new ways. People are complex and ever-changing. The good counselor must balance clear direction while also remaining fluid, watching and listening for the larger story. This is a hallmark of interest.

DEDICATED TO SAVING A MARRIAGE

Recently, I listened to a doctor who performed surgeries on very sick patients. When asked if he ever felt discouraged, he said, "I am hopeful with every surgery I do. While I'm a realist and convey truth to my patients, I'm hopeful that there is always something I can do to assist healing, no matter how small it may be."

This is the kind of attitude the good marriage counselor has and is able to convey to their clients. Of course, for the counselor, there is reason to hope by virtue of the fact that the couple has shown up to work on their marriage.

The good counselor, trained and educated, with a specialty in marriage counseling and a genuine interest in their client, adds a layer of sincerity and dedication to the cause of saving a marriage. They have chosen to specialize in marriage counseling, working with both spouses together and separately to help them achieve their goals. This quality of dedication is seen and felt by the client.

Remember, the client often comes to the counseling process having previous negative experiences with counseling, and they are living in a troubled relationship. Hope is usually in short supply. Finding a dedicated counselor can feel like a lifesaver in desperate times.

CULTIVATING COMPASSION AND RAPPORT

Closely related to showing genuine interest in the client and being dedicated to helping save the marriage is the need for compassion. A counselor can be skilled in the techniques of marriage counseling, but if they lack compassion, they are not likely to develop a rapport with the client.

Sensing whether a counselor has compassion is a relatively straightforward endeavor. Does the counselor show an emotional connection and understanding with the client? Are they able to convey that understanding, perhaps from their own experience or having had similar counseling experiences in the past? Clients want to work with someone who is relatable; the client is looking to create a form a connection with their counselor.

Good counseling cannot exist without ongoing rapport between client and counselor. Technically, rapport means having a sense that two people—or three in the case of marriage counseling—understand each other's feelings and communicate effectively.

Having rapport with your counselor is critical. Because it can be difficult to convey one's experience, the counselor must work to understand exactly where the client is coming from and what they are trying to share. The good counselor understands their client and communicates this effectively. When done correctly, rapport and trust will be built between them.

CLEAR AND COMPELLING DIRECTION

Education, specialized training, and supervised experience are foundational to being a good marriage counselor. We've considered the importance of compassion and rapport as well. Still more is needed.

The effective counselor offers clear and compelling direction. Gone are the days when you would lie on a couch while the counselor sat and listened compassionately. We all appreciate someone who will listen to us share our heartaches. But this is not enough when your marriage is in trouble.

When your marriage is in jeopardy, you want a lifesaver. You want an emergency room doctor who will roll up their sleeves, call out "Code Blue," and pull out all of their tools to save the marriage. Marriage counseling is not the time for a passive counselor who simply asks, "How are you?" and reflects back what you've answered.

This truth has taken me some time to understand. It has taken years of experience to recognize the depth of pain and the urgency with which most couples come for counseling. They are not looking for a listening ear, as important as that is. They are looking for more than kindness and compassion. *They are looking for direction.* They know something is dreadfully wrong, and they want, sometimes even demand, answers.

A couple must find and work with a counselor who is gifted in offering clear, compelling instruction, someone willing to hear difficult things and willing to make bold decisions. The dynamic counselor is engaging, exudes confidence, and is able to communicate the path forward. The good marriage counselor is one part teacher, one part encourager, and one part firefighter, working to stop an emotional inferno between two people.

> A TROUBLED COUPLE MUST FIND A COUNSELOR WHO IS GIFTED IN OFFERING CLEAR, COMPELLING INSTRUCTION, SOMEONE WHO CAN HEAR DIFFICULT THINGS AND MAKE BOLD DECISIONS.

The skilled counselor is able to communicate why couples are stuck and how to help them become healthier. The instruction must be compelling, perhaps even urgent, given to couples in such a way that they are motivated to participate in the healing solution. The couple in distress appreciates a strong, assertive, confident counselor willing to say hard things in an atmosphere of compassion and kindness.

KEEN INSIGHTS AND SKILLED AT ASSESSMENT

The counselor—the couple's teacher, encourager, and firefighter— must also be wise, skilled in offering insights and making accurate assessments of a troubled marriage. This requires more than an average clinician. It takes a Red Adair.

Paul Neal "Red" Adair was an oil well firefighter who became internationally famous for his highly specialized skills and ability to extinguish and cap oil well blowouts. Born and raised in the oil country of Texas, Red was called upon to go into the most volatile, dangerous situations to save lives and money.

You may think I exaggerate when I compare marriage counseling to capping explosive oil wells. I assure you, some marriage situations are akin to fiery explosions and require confidence, keen insights, and accurate assessments. Effective marriage counseling even requires bravery to tackle situations many shy away from.

A thoroughly trained and experienced counselor will be able to offer perceptive observations regarding complex problems. No one wants a mediocre professional, but rather wants to know that the person with whom they entrust their marriage has the requisite skills to lead them forward. It isn't enough to merely have those skills, however; they must also have the ability to convey those skills.

So, we're back to the question of finding the Red Adair of counseling. I suggest you will know you've met this kind of counselor when they have all the skills we've discussed so far, plus *confidence!*

The good marriage counselor *knows* they are a good counselor. They've been practicing long enough that they know their stuff. They've studied enough, trained enough, been supervised enough, and practiced enough so they are able to convey that they have the ability to help you with your most difficult situation.

When you meet this person, and spend any time with them, you will walk away feeling assured they are up to the task. You might be put off just a bit by their confidence, perhaps mistaking it as swagger, but in time, you'll see they are simply confident—and that is what you need.

INTERVENTION

After deftly defining the couple's problems and beginning to solve the complex emotional and relational puzzle, the skilled counselor must intervene. After all, if they simply listen, even with compassion, they will not have interrupted the destructive patterns that are hurting the marriage.

The good counselor has a number of interventions in their arsenal of tools. Having read and trained extensively, having supervision on complex cases, they know where and how to intervene. They know how to name and confront problems and the impact these issues are having on the individuals and the marriage, even when such intervention is resisted.

Another way a good counselor might intervene is to help the client recognize and amplify the things they are doing right. This is known as *solution-focused counseling.* While not all counselors need to embrace this specific counseling skill, tenets from this practice need to be woven into the client's work.

The value of solution-focused work lies in focusing on positive things the client is already doing, as opposed to seeing only the problems. Clients typically come to counseling riveted on their problems. This is very understandable. However, the good counselor knows these clients are overlooking many times when they have done things right and they need to recognize these moments of growth.

Can you see the change in focus? Good counselors must help their clients construct solutions to their problems and learn how to rehearse those solutions. This is often a radical and powerful shift in focus and has been proven very effective in bringing about change.

This model of effective counseling shifts from confrontation and interpretation to discovering the places and ways the client is already functioning effectively. Imagine the goodwill this engenders between client and counselor, typically offering the counselor the trust needed to encourage further growth.

CHALLENGE TO GROW

Any intervention requires boldness to confront maladaptive behavior that resists necessary change. An intervention requires urgency, clarifying why and what is imperative to change.

ANY INTERVENTION REQUIRES BOLDNESS TO CONFRONT MALADAPTIVE BEHAVIOR THAT RESISTS NECESSARY CHANGE.

Typically, such confrontation is met with at least some resistance. Still, the confident and skilled counselor holds fast to the necessary direction, making the consequences of not changing very clear. Additionally, the confident counselor clarifies that staying stuck leads to further unhappiness in the marriage, while facing change leads to ultimate peace.

These can be very difficult moments in marriage counseling.

I spoke with a drug and alcohol counselor recently about his work. I expected him to offer a long and complicated journey to freedom from drug and alcohol abuse and addiction. He offered quite the opposite.

"What special skills are needed to help someone get clean and sober?" I asked, suspecting a change of this magnitude to be extremely complicated.

"No special skills," he said, almost nonchalantly. "Someone has to decide not to put the marijuana pipe up to their mouth, not to put the straw containing cocaine up to their nose. They have to not take a drink."

"That's it?" I asked, somewhat incredulous.

"That's it," he said confidently. "I can tell how motivated someone is about growing and changing in the first few minutes of meeting them. It can certainly be a difficult path to get clean and sober, but not as complex as we make it out to be."

I found his perspective refreshing and reflected on my work as a marriage counselor. Marriage counseling often contains the same candor. Good counselors point out the arrogance, immaturity, and patterns of damaging behavior, and help the clients see these and take ownership of them. They point out ways the couple are acting that cause severe damage, making their choices clearer. The rest is up to the couple.

GOOD COUNSELORS CARE

A complacent counselor does the bare minimum and seems to lack the energy to help the couple. The good counselor brings an excitement, enthusiasm, and genuine caring to the counseling session.

How might a good counselor show that they care?

Good Counselors Show Caring by Attention

While this may seem to go without saying, that is not the case. Offering undivided attention is as much an art as it is a skill. The good counselor creates the emotional and literal space to sit and *listen* to you. Their phone doesn't ring, there is no knock on the door, and the chairs are placed in such a way that you know you have their undivided attention. Such attention is healing.

Good Counselors Show Caring by Asking Good Questions

The good counselor, having established undivided physical and emotional presence, asks about you—not one question, but *many* questions in an attempt to get the full picture of your story. The counselor knows it takes time, attention, and asking very specific questions to unravel the mystery of someone's life. As they listen, they know the next question, and the next, to arrive at a complete understanding of a person's dilemma.

Good Counselors Show Caring by Accurate Empathy

The good counselor knows to layer their keen listening and questions with accurate empathy, which is the ability to describe and feel another's experience. This personal empathy has a healing impact. It has been said that listening for understanding is a key component of love. We all know that having someone's attention, leading to accurate empathy, is powerful.

Good Counselors Show Caring by Remembering

Good counselors know it is painful to have to share a story again and again. Couples in distress don't want to have to repeat what they've already shared. They want to get the sense that the counselor has listened so intently that they bring their understanding forward, from one session to the next. Remembering a client's story is a powerful way of showing the client you care about what they are sharing with you.

Good Counselors Show Caring by Feeling Appropriate Righteous Indignation

Clients want their counselor to speak out against bad behavior. Wrong is wrong, and clients want their counselor to care enough that they speak out boldly against wrongful, hurtful, and harmful actions.

This goes against the training of some counselors who shield their reactions behind the notion they must always remain impartial. While it is certainly true the good counselor is unbiased, at some point, they must weigh in on issues presented to them. Speaking out against harm done by either spouse is another powerful way to show that the counselor is emotionally involved and will advocate for one or the other when appropriate.

Good Counselors Have Genuine Curiosity

All too often, the mediocre, complacent counselor settles for what is said to them. The good counselor not only asks pointed, even piercing, questions but maintains an attitude of curiosity.

> GOOD COUNSELORS ARE DRIVEN BY GENTLE CURIOSITY, WHICH KEEPS THEM ENGAGED AND ATTACHED TO THE COUPLE SO THAT THEIR STRATEGIC ALLIANCE IS MAINTAINED.

This gentle curiosity is a driving force within the good counselor. Good counselors know they are sitting with a giant jigsaw puzzle, with each piece fitting into a picture that they cannot yet finish. The mysterious story of this couple is revealed, one piece of information at a time, and the counselor is motivated by curiosity. It is this same curiosity that motivates the counselor to keep asking questions, even as they begin to form conclusions.

Why might a counselor continue to ask questions even after they have begun to form an opinion about what is happening with the couple sitting with them? Because certainty leads to rigid perceptions, which impedes the counselor's curiosity. Certainty can lead to presumptions and emotional laziness.

Think about it. If the counselor *knows* what is happening, they'll stop asking questions. They'll stop being curious, and the client will sense this disengagement. Curiosity keeps the counselor engaged and attached to the client. It is part of the fuel needed to maintain the strategic alliance we discussed in the last chapter.

ATTENTION AND ACTIVE LISTENING

There is a vast difference between listening and active listening. We've all experienced someone who is able to parrot back to us what we've been saying while adding nothing to the conversation.

The complacent counselor listens for what is being said, perhaps even rephrasing what they've heard, but adds nothing substantial to the conversation. In contrast, the good counselor listens with curiosity, always searching for what is alive in this couple. What are their deepest concerns? They not only listen for what is being said, they wonder about what is *not* being said. They ask probing questions, offer reflections, and perhaps even add stories from their own life that help to clarify the current issues.

The good counselor wonders about what is alive in each of their clients, both individually and as a couple. To find the answers takes genuine caring, active listening, and unyielding curiosity.

There is listening…and then there is listening to understand deeper issues. We all feel the difference. Attentive, active listening is giving your undivided, undistracted attention to a person. It's noticing this other person and the nuances that make them a unique individual. We reflect back, with our gestures, inflections, and nonverbal cues, showing our attachment to what they are saying.

Giving someone our complete attention means we listen not only to the words they are saying but also pay attention to their meaning. The good counselor listens for the story they are telling and considers its implications and significance. The counselor knows the client has come to them with a deep longing in their hearts, a desire to be truly heard that they have likely not had for a long time.

This kind of intentional listening takes a great deal of energy. The counselor must be focused, intent on hearing the deeper story. Both client and counselor will know when that connection has taken place.

To truly hear the deeper story the counselor must be free from distractions. M. Scott Peck wrote about this idea when he explained the concept of "bracketing" in his book *The Road Less Traveled*. To listen to the deeper meaning in a person's heart, Peck said, means to bracket or set aside any reactions, rebuttals, or challenges, so that there's space to allow the client's story to emerge.

Bracketing makes sense when we think about listening, because having a reaction, perhaps even a rebuttal, is a natural response. Bracketing, setting aside your own agenda, is actually unnatural. Bracketing, really hearing the client, is an acquired skill. When done correctly, a powerful bond takes place between speaker and listener, client and counselor.

Something even more, however, is needed for good counseling.

God is our model of compassionate listening. We see this in Scripture as God hears the laments and cries of the Hebrew people. In the book of Exodus, we discover a God who truly listens as His people cry out with heavy groans. God is so compassionate that when the Hebrew people are freed from bondage in Egypt, a community of faith is established in Israel. God instructs the leaders to call the people of God together on a regular basis for the practice of lamentation. This social and spiritual practice was an intentional and public way of making visible the reality of grief and suffering. God knew the people needed a way to come together to share their emotional and spiritual pain with one another.

Compassionate listening is an absolute necessity for a good counselor. No couple whose marriage is failing wants complacence. They need to feel the counselor's engagement, concern, and compassion.

COLLABORATIVE COUNSELING

Complacent counselors set their course early in the counseling and rarely veer from that course. They are rigid, limited in their skills.

In contrast, the good counselor is versatile, flexible, and nimble. They set a course but then shift directions when necessary. They have many tools at their disposal and are ready to use them.

Like the physician who seeks to define the medical problem, intervenes with a solution, and then *checks in* with the patient, so too the effective counselor is always seeking information as to the success of their interventions. They are ready to *stay the course* or change directions to ensure their counsel is as beneficial as possible.

Once a counselor becomes complacent, they are no longer actively listening. They've become lazy in their problem/definition/remedy cycle. The good counselor is always revising their definition of the problem based upon the feedback they receive from the client.

There is no *one size fits all*. The good counselor constantly asks if what they're doing is working. They are focused on ensuring their counseling is aligning with the client's needs. This begins at the first meeting and continues in subsequent sessions as the counselor and client assess each other. Do I have the skills to address this client's needs? Does the client sense their needs align with what the counselor has to offer?

The good counselor knows that alignment of values and focus doesn't always occur and must be ready to refer the client to someone else more qualified or better able to meet their needs. Alignment is not a once-and-for-all process. The good counselor is always checking in with the client to ensure movement in the direction the client wants.

CLARITY, INDECISION, AND COHESION

Clients are desperate for solutions. They want clear direction and a cohesive understanding of their problems. Even if the path forward is challenging, many couples will choose it when offered clear, cohesive direction and hope for change.

The good counselor takes their time in assessing the situation and then, at the right time and in the right way, offers a clear, cohesive path forward. The counselor has listened intently, has shown compassion and understanding, has shown empathy, and has aligned themselves with the client. Now, when it is time to offer a treatment plan, the counselor does so with thorough professionalism.

To do this means the counselor knows what they are doing. They have the requisite training and experience to step into a chaotic situation and offer order. Utilizing all of their abilities, they confidently state what they see happening before them and suggest an appropriate plan of action.

The good counselor also sits on a fence of sorts, with one half leaning on knowledge of what they see and what they believe needs to be done, and the other half leaning away and sitting with indecision. Clarity will come in time to the hard-working couple and counselor.

And what about the role of hope and meaning in the journey?

HOPE AND MEANING FOR THE JOURNEY

In addition to focused, compassionate listening and knowledgeable planning, the good counselor must offer hope and meaning for the couple's struggles. Without hope, we all have a tendency to give up.

Beleaguered clients, like Garrett and Kara, typically arrive at counseling feeling hopeless. Kara came to their first session with the good counselor very apprehensive, without much hope that this would be better than their previous counseling experiences.

A good counselor recognizes this absence of hope. This is where the counseling must begin—with the previous challenges in counseling. The good counselor notes this absence of hope and finds special opportunities to offer encouragement.

Encouragement and hope are not enough, however. The good counselor finds ways to weave meaning into the client's journey. The counselor helps the couple find purpose in this journey. Every challenge faced by a client is, in a real sense, an opportunity for growth, and it is up to the counselor to walk the client through this process. Finding meaning in the struggle transforms it from something unbearable to something they can actually embrace.

> **A GOOD COUNSELOR RECOGNIZES A COUPLE'S ABSENCE OF HOPE AND FINDS SPECIAL OPPORTUNITIES TO OFFER ENCOURAGEMENT.**

PUTTING IT ALL TOGETHER

An effective counselor is in a very important and critical position. They have the opportunity to bring hope to a seemingly hopeless situation, encouragement to a discouraged couple. This counselor must be skilled and have the ability to create a clear path forward.

Can you see how much talent is needed to be a good counselor? This profession is not for someone unwilling to journey into complicated places with their clients. This work is not for someone wanting quick and easy solutions, for those rarely exist.

No, the good counselor has many, many skills and a strong sense of intuition, for there will be many times when the counselor must listen to their heart. Textbook answers won't help in many of the complex situations that exist in marriage counseling. There are times when a counselor relies as much on their intuition as on their training. They *read* the client and move forward boldly, with a dose of uncertainty.

All of the skills discussed in this chapter are needed to be a good counselor. A bright, energetic counselor without compassion is of little value to the client in desperate need of care and consideration. The compassionate counselor who only listens, but lacks other skills, will disappoint most clients.

The good counselor knows how to actively listen, show compassion and empathy, align their skills with the needs of the client, and have the confidence to outline an effective path forward, again and again as is necessary.

CLOSING THOUGHTS

I have been a counselor for over forty years and do not regret a day of it. It is a challenging and rewarding career. When looking back over the years, I see that my clients have often been my best teachers. While schooling was instrumental in launching my career, the hours spent in the consulting room have been where I've made the mistakes that have taught me more effective ways to really help couples.

I've also come to appreciate that marriage counseling is much more difficult than I originally thought. Although it's incredibly rewarding, it is definitely not easy work. I've learned I must always seek better and more effective ways to intervene in complex situations.

I've learned that couples can simultaneously be desperate for help and firmly attached to their old ways of doing things. I've come to appreciate that people, ultimately, must find their own way. I'm a guide, but only a guide.

So, it is my job, and the job of all good counselors, not to be discouraged by the lack of progress, but to continually ask ourselves what we can do better, what we can do differently, to help a couple. We must learn their language and hope they will, in the end, learn ours too.

Having learned what constitutes a good counselor, let's consider good marriage counseling. How should good marriage counseling work? Let's explore this together.

PRELUDE:
BRIANNE AND KENT

"What do you think? How do you feel about him?" Brianne asked her husband Kent as they left the counselor's office.

"Well, counseling's not really my thing," he said, "but I've got to admit, I feel a little better about it after talking to this guy."

"Me, too," Brianne said. "What do you think he said that made you feel so encouraged?"

"That's a great question," Kent answered. "I'm not sure. I was ready to feel the same way about this guy that I felt about the woman we saw a year ago. She left me with a bad feeling. But today, I feel encouraged."

"I was anxious about how it would go too," Brianne said. "We should give ourselves a little credit though. We did a lot of research this time before we made an appointment."

"That last experience wasn't good," Kent said. "She didn't listen to us the way this guy did. She didn't ask any hard questions the way this guy did. I liked his combination of being tough, but caring."

"He is totally different from anyone we've seen before," Brianne said. "You're right about the questions. Some were pretty challenging. I wasn't sure about his direction at first, but I have to admit he made me think and he had some good insights."

"I have to say I was happy he kept asking you tough questions," Kent chuckled. "I was afraid he was only going to challenge me, and I was glad he was just as tough on you as he was on me. He seemed equally involved with both of us."

"What did you think when he asked us about our previous counseling?" Brianne asked. "That was an uncomfortable moment for me. I didn't want to say anything bad about that last one. She was nice enough, but she just didn't seem to care about us."

"I'm sure he's had people who didn't like him, too," Kent said. "I don't think we said anything negative about her, other than she didn't help us. This guy's ready to help us, and I know it sounds weird, but I think he knows how to get us where we need to go. That's huge."

"What else did you think about him?" Brianne asked.

"He was friendly," Kent said, "but I felt he still got down to business. I like how relaxed he made me feel. He let us know that he's heard stories like ours before. I liked that. He wasn't shocked by anything we said and at times it was like he could read our minds. There were a couple of times when he added more to what I said, and he was right on. That caught my attention."

"It was kind of strange when he asked about our parents the way he did," Brianne said. "It was like he saw some of our patterns and figured out we might have learned some bad habits from them. Do you remember me looking over at you when he first asked about them?"

"Yeah," Kent said. "He's definitely had a lot of experience at this. You could tell by his insights. I don't remember any of the counselors making those kinds of connections. I think we made a good choice. I'm kind of looking forward to working together with him on our problems. I feel like he cares, is fair, and will help us get where we need to go."

"I think so too," Brianne said. "He's going to push us, but I guess that's what we need. We've needed someone who is passionate about their work and really invested in helping couples like us."

"We better get ready to so some real work," Kent said.

"I really appreciate you doing this, Kent," Brianne added. "I know counseling is not your thing and this is stretching you. But, it means a lot to me. Together we can use this counseling to make us grow."

"Thanks," Kent said. "This guy is good at his job. I need to be stretched. I don't have much experience being this vulnerable around people. I've not been open like this to very many people, but I trust him. I'll give it a good effort."

"That encourages me," Brianne said.

GOOD MARRIAGE COUNSELING

Behind every happy couple lies two people who have fought
hard to overcome all obstacles and interference to be that way.
Why? Because it's what they wanted.
—Kim George

Good. Marriage. Counseling. Not often do you hear these three words together. They might even be considered an oxymoron. It's a little bit like saying, "Good stomach surgery."

Yet they should be words heard together frequently. There certainly is an extraordinary need for good marriage counseling. Most couples experience significant conflict at different points in their relationship and desperately need good marriage counseling.

Thankfully, in spite of the many negative experiences, there really is such a thing as *good marriage counseling.*

We read how Kent and Brianne researched and discovered a strong marriage counselor. It wasn't blind luck that led them to their new counselor. Knowledge gained from bad counseling experiences, combined with challenging research, helped them make a wise choice.

In this chapter, we'll merge what you learned about why marriage counseling fails and the qualities of a good marriage counselor to answer these questions:

+ What does positive marriage counseling look like?

+ How should the counseling process unfold?

+ What are some signs of marriage counseling done well?

Learning the answers to these questions will give you even more insights into what to look for in a good marriage counseling process. These answers will help you make wise choices as you seek good marriage counseling.

THE INVITATION

Entering into marriage counseling is a momentous experience. Consider that couples entering this process are in a vulnerable state, with high hopes and equally high fears and trepidation. They are unsure of what will be asked of them, what will be exposed in them, and what will be expected of them in the counseling process.

With emotions running high, believing their marriage is in trouble, they walk through the counselor's door, hoping beyond hope that they've chosen the right person to lead them from conflict to connection, detachment to engagement.

With this clearly in mind, the good counselor invites the clients to enter into the counseling process. This invitation to be vulnerable and embrace change is frightening for the client. In many respects, a marriage is truly in jeopardy, and the counselor is being sought for their expertise and ability to guide a couple who have clearly lost their way.

Because this process is so critical, the counselor must begin with a generous, gracious, and kind invitation. Any preliminary phone consultation taking place before the appointment should be treated with utmost dignity and sensitivity because this is the beginning of the invitation to counseling.

Whether the initial contact is with the counselor or the appointment staff, everyone must be mindful of the importance of this initial invitation to counseling. If a staff member is handling the initial call, they must be trained to understand the importance of making the potential client feel at ease, answer questions, and begin to clarify expectations.

Seeking counseling is a huge step. Most often, the couple places the call out of desperation. This is a last resort. They feel hopeless. If they've tried counseling before and found it to be unhelpful or hurtful, they feel even more trepidation. The counselor and the counselor's staff must appreciate this vulnerability and do everything to reassure the client, showing understanding of the trust being placed in them.

> **REASSURANCE AND CLEAR INFORMATION, OFFERED WITH COMPASSION AND UNDERSTANDING, WILL DO MUCH TO INITIATE A GOOD COUNSELING PROCESS.**

The counselor or counseling staff recognizes this initial phone call as a plea for help. This request for services is an invitation into the client's frightening experience, and the good counselor responds to this invitation to assist them. Reassurance and clear information, offered with compassion and understanding, will do much to initiate a good counseling process. Whether the couple has been to counseling before or not, this is a new person, a new time in their lives, and a new experience. It is daunting.

THE ROLE OF EMOTIONS

Since the initial venture into counseling is typically fraught with emotions such as fear, the good marriage counselor and their staff are mindful of the interplay between emotions and decisions.

Consider the role of fear in this initial counseling process. Most individuals entering into marriage counseling have significant doubts about being heard and understood. They don't want to be made to feel ashamed of where they are in their marriage. The effective counselor reminds themselves of that fear and takes extra steps of precaution so the client's questions are answered, their fears—both spoken and unspoken—are addressed, and the client is helped to make wise choices.

In an article titled "The Best Way to Make Decisions When You're Emotional – Is to Not Make Them," Hamnah Amir writes:

> Emotion has the ability to overpower our senses and functions. When this happens, we are prone to making poor decisions… [Fear] decreases the likelihood of risk-averse choices. Keep in mind that when people are afraid of something, they often become angry.[15]

What does this have to do with the counselor's role and function? This is a delicate time in the good marriage counseling process. This initial invitation sets the stage for future good work to occur by the counselor being especially gentle, understanding, and kind. The counselor must work especially hard to clarify expectations.

AGREED-UPON EXPECTATIONS

Fear and trepidation create an atmosphere where so many possibilities for miscommunications exist. The good marriage counselor recognizes that the counseling has begun even while setting up an initial appointment, or answering questions about the counseling. Building rapport and establishing trust occur from the earliest invitation.

There are so many possibilities for miscommunications, misunderstandings, and feelings of disappointment. When expectations are amiss, problems occur, and if not immediately rectified, the entire counseling process can be derailed.

---

15. Hamnah Amir, "The Best Way to Make Decisions When You're Emotional – Is to Not Make Them," *Psychreg*, July 12, 2020 (www.psychreg.org/decisions-when-emotional).

Along with the client's request for help comes a list of expectations; the success of marriage counseling hinges on an agreement of these expectations. Good counseling begins with establishing clear boundaries about the problem focus, length of sessions, frequency of sessions, and the roles of counselor and client. What is expected of the counselor and what is expected of the client must be clearly established.

Remember Kara and Garrett's negative experience? Their expectations were not met, and this nearly cost them the possibility of working things out with another counselor. Their last counselor missed an opportunity to clarify expectations; subsequently, Kara and Garrett didn't return to that counselor.

Good counseling involves both client and counselor, defining expectations up-front and clearly. However, the problem lies in knowing exactly what the clients need and teaching them how they can ask for something different in the counseling process. To expect clients to walk in the door with a clear set of expectations is unrealistic. This places the responsibility on the shoulders of the counselor to know how to explore expectations.

A POWERFUL, FRAGILE ALLIANCE

Although the relationship between client and counselor is a mutual process, the responsibility for good marriage counseling falls first and foremost on the counselor. The counselor is the one to note, understand, and manage the fears and concerns of the client.

I have always been impressed at the kindness of my dentist and his dental staff, though I still resist going to the dentist. These professionals understand me. They know I'm anxious before I even sit down in the dental chair. They anticipate my anxiety without my saying a word. So, they do everything possible to make me comfortable—from the music they play, the receptionist's greeting, the gentleness of the dental assistant, and so on to the dentist. Each of these steps plays a role in creating a positive alliance. I know that the staff is there for one purpose: to help me with my dental health.

The marriage counselor is also there for one purpose: to assist you in regaining your marital health. Mindful of the client's anxiety, they must create an atmosphere of trust. Mindful there is too much at stake to take any part of this process for granted, a good counselor reassures the client that their welfare comes first and foremost. The counselor knows if any part of the process doesn't convey complete trust and competence, the client will not return. Furthermore, they may never visit another counselor.

> # A GOOD COUNSELOR KNOWS IF ANY PART OF THE PROCESS DOESN'T CONVEY COMPLETE TRUST AND COMPETENCE, THE CLIENT WILL NOT RETURN.

The therapeutic alliance is made up of two parts, the couple and the counselor. If either one fails to fulfill their role, all is lost. When all participants do their part, there can be positive growth.

It is often helpful to remember, and be reminded, that *we're in this together, and we can figure this out.* There is power in acknowledging and believing we are a team with a purpose. Together, we have a mission: to save a marriage.

But make no mistake, this alliance of counselor and client is incredibly fragile. Trust can be broken in so many ways, sending the client running. The counselor must be ever mindful of the fragility of this professional partnership, understanding that the client is likely very anxious about this difficult work. The counselor must avoid errors such as misspoken words and overly harsh confrontations, as these will not be well-received. Although the counselor does not intend to hurt the client's feelings, it can happen easily, and trust may be broken. Broken trust in any relationship is not quickly repaired.

MAINTAINING THE PROFESSIONAL CONNECTION

Good counseling only occurs when the alliance, the professional partnership, is maintained. Good counseling, as we've learned, is a fragile connection, a serious, trusting, collaborative partnership. It can be broken in myriad ways. It must be constantly maintained.

The counselor continually reminds the client that this counseling process is a collaborative effort, with a common goal of saving their marriage. Progress cannot be made unless all parties work together toward this goal.

The good counselor must be constantly mindful of this tenuous connection, sensitive to the fact that the couple is entrusting their marriage to this professional and has high expectations. This truth is kept in the forefront of the good marriage counselor's mind.

What if the client's expectations are excessive? The counselor must address all expectations because to avoid them means risking tension in the partnership. The counselor brings expectations to the foreground where they can be discussed and makes it clear why some expectations can't be fulfilled. Even this process of talking about expectations can be healing. Issues are talked about in safety, with opinions valued, concerns addressed, and solutions explored.

It is this emotional dance, the dialogue between client and counselor about expectations, that reinforces a powerful alliance that must be monitored and maintained by the counselor. When the partnership is shaken, perhaps due to expectations not being met, the good counselor works to restore trust by talking out the issues.

In a healthy counseling process, the client learns that issues can be discussed safely and effectively. No issue has to be pushed aside, dismissed, or left unspoken. No issue is ignored or assumed to be unimportant.

What can be done when the counselor or client senses some issues are not being discussed? What can be done to make sure the unspoken issues are brought to the foreground, where they can be explored?

MAKING THE UNSPOKEN SPOKEN

Good counseling involves a counselor who is tenacious and willing to pursue important issues hiding in the background. The couple comes to counseling because too many expectations, hurt feelings, and issues have not been adequately discussed between them. Unresolved problems have gone underground, where hurt feelings fester and resentment grows. Avoidance of issues usually leads to resentment, which leads to disconnection.

Good counseling is an opportunity to change those destructive patterns. In a sense, it's an illustration of how good communication can happen. Issues are not avoided in the counseling relationship, so this relationship feels different. Here, unspoken issues become spoken. Feelings and concerns between client and counselor are addressed.

Noticing unspoken expectations and feelings takes an incredibly watchful eye on the part of the counselor. The client is likely to exhibit an unhealthy way of processing feelings, either by stuffing them, acting them out, or exploding at the counselor. The counselor must show a healthier way of interacting, modeling more effective communication.

Clients are not likely to be completely open about their hurts and disappointments, so the counselor must probe for these concerns. Clients are often not inclined, or skilled, at speaking about their concerns with the counseling itself either. They will complain about their mate, but are not likely to complain about the counseling. So again, it is the responsibility of the counselor to watch what takes place and make the unspoken spoken.

REALIGNMENT OF EXPECTATIONS

Since clients will not typically make their goals clear, good counseling involves an ongoing realignment of expectations. It's not a subject to raise only during the initial session. Rather, the good counselor will discuss the couple's expectations with them as a matter of course.

How does this occur? Just as spouses in a healthy marriage check in with one another routinely, the good counselor checks in with the client regularly to see if their expectations are being met. The client will appreciate this concern and will now be much more likely to offer their feelings and concerns about the counseling process.

> **THE COUNSELOR MUST NOT ONLY HELP THE COUPLE WITH THEIR ISSUES, BUT ALSO MAKE SURE THAT THE PROCESS IS WORKING FOR THEM AND THEIR EXPECTATIONS ARE BEING MET.**

Close monitoring of the counseling process involves the counselor not only working on the presenting marital issues, but also watching the emotional connection between counselor and client. This watchfulness should involve *checking in*, where observations are made and clarification is sought. This is best done with clear questions, such as:

- How are you feeling about our counseling process?
- Do you have any concerns?
- Is there anything you'd like me to do differently?
- Are your expectations of counseling being met?

These simple, straightforward questions are likely to yield invaluable information or possibly lead to further discussion. Good counseling involves continuously evaluating the counseling process and being willing to adjust it when necessary.

MAKING THE MOST OF COUNSELING

There are ways to help the client be "a good client," and things the client can do to make the counseling process more effective. It's possible to be a better client and have more positive experiences in the counseling process simply by having better communication. It's also critical to be clear about what the counseling process can give to you, what you must give to it, and what you should expect from it.

In an article titled "8 Ways to Make the Most of Counseling,"[16] Marci Payne offers these eight tips for doing your part to create a positive counseling experience:

1. Be Honest

Not only is it critical to be honest with your counselor about what is happening in your life, but it's just as critical to be *honest with yourself* about what is happening. Denial is a great protective barrier we all use at times, but it keeps us from growing. The client must be encouraged and challenged not to hold back. Honesty and candor help to determine what is happening in the counseling process, and what may need to be changed.

2. Identify Counseling Goals

It is imperative to have clear counseling goals and expectations that are aligned with what your counselor has promised. These goals must be specific and clear. It is helpful to understand and state your motivations for these goals. The more powerful the motivations, the more likely the goals will be maintained.

Good counseling is not a passive process but an active relationship where the client specifies goals. The good counselor listens and understands the client's goals; together, they can monitor whether these goals are being fulfilled.

3. Keep a Counseling Journal

Writing down goals and counseling takeaways is a powerful way to make the process even more robust. Talking out problems with a counselor is helpful, but writing about them, expanding on them, and perhaps even sharing them with another person is a way to make the experience more practical and alive.

---

16. Marci Payne, "8 Ways to Make the Most of Counseling," *Talkspace*, August 8, 2016 (www.talkspace.com/blog/8-ways-to-make-the-most-of-counseling).

4. Prepare for Sessions

It's important to consider and plan ahead of time what you want to have happen in a counseling session. Clients must think about what they want to accomplish in every session and come prepared to talk about those issues.

Too frequently, couples come to their session tempted to talk about the argument of the day or week. While this may be on the top of their mind and their greatest concern at the moment, it is not likely the most meaningful thing to be talked about. Preparation involves reflecting ahead of time on patterns of interactions, stuck points as well as points of success. Consideration must be given as to how current issues fit into long-term patterns that the couple wishes to change.

5. Speak Up Before Ending Counseling

As I've said, couples typically share feelings about counseling indirectly, by attending sessions and participating fully, or by dropping out of counseling. This does not give the counselor an opportunity to adjust their processes, and it leaves the client with a poor investment of their time and energies. So, speak up. Let the counselor know when you are tempted to stop counseling and why. Bring your concerns. The good marriage counselor will appreciate the openness.

6. Recognize That the Therapist Will Not "Fix" You or Tell You What to Do

Many counselors take a passive approach to the counseling process and expect the client to find their own solutions. While there is certainly value to this approach, I *do* think there are times when direct guidance is appropriate. While a counselor should not tell a client what they *must* do, there are times when it is appropriate to tell a client that the path they've chosen is not likely to get them where they want to go, and alternate plans may be more beneficial.

7. Keep Counseling at Least Somewhat Private

Resist the urge to use your counseling to fix other people. The counseling you receive is tailored specifically for your own growth, not to change your mate or anyone else. You should not attempt to align others with your position. Focus must be maintained on what you are gaining from the counseling and how you can be a more effective partner in the marriage.

8. Try Mental Health Prevention

You don't have to wait until you are experiencing a crisis to reach out for help. In fact, after the current crisis diminishes may be the best time to really dig in to determine how to prevent a crisis in the future. Mental health prevention involves considering how to avoid potential trouble. When you're not sure what to talk about, this can be the perfect time to more calmly explore patterns of interacting that led to a crisis or might lead to one in the future.

SUPPORT/CONFRONTATION BALANCE

Good counseling must maintain a balance of support and confrontation. This is typically hard to achieve. The good counselor is mindful of doing their job while monitoring the fragile alliance between counselor and client. This is a dynamic relationship often occurring in the midst of feelings of desperation and discouragement.

If the client receives too much support in counseling, the client is not likely to gain much from the process. While there is value in feeling encouraged and cared for, they will not be challenged to change. However, if the counselor continually confronts the client, the client will feel overly challenged and will likely retreat in an effort of self-protection.

It is not enough for the counselor to support and confront. The client must *feel* both supported and confronted by the counselor. The client is typically sensitive, having likely endured a great deal of conflict already. They now come to a professional to *feel* not only that this person cares about them but also is encouraging them to grow.

Good counseling, then, is a fine balance between these two needs, a delicate combination of support and confrontation, encouragement and challenge. If this balance is jeopardized, the client will typically retreat.

GOOD COUNSELING IS A FINE BALANCE BETWEEN SUPPORT AND CONFRONTATION, ENCOURAGEMENT AND CHALLENGE.

It takes a keen counselor who *reads* when this balance is achieved. The good counselor monitors how well the client tolerates being challenged and assesses how much support the client needs. When this balance is achieved, good counseling occurs. Balancing support and challenge is perhaps the counselor's hardest job.

While there are dangers at both ends of the spectrum, the effective counselor teaches the client that for growth to occur, they must be challenged. Good counseling stretches the client, creating a safe place to grow and try out new attitudes and behaviors.

This is what makes counseling both an art and a science, creating a perfect teaching opportunity.

THE EXCELLENT TEACHER

My piano teacher is a modern-day Mary Poppins in that she adheres to the principle, "Just a spoonful of sugar helps the medicine go down." Claire does this by encouraging me to keep working on a hard piece of music and ultimately applying gold stars to the piece passing her inspection.

To be clear, before achieving the gold star, I must rehearse a piece of music for weeks. Claire will have critiqued my piano playing numerous times, taught me tricks for reading the music, and new ways to hold my hands on the keyboard.

The effective counseling process is similar. The good counselor is a good teacher. Through the balance of support and confrontation, encouragement and challenge, the counselor inspires the client to keep growing. The counselor teaches the client to anticipate tough patches of work and encourages them not to give up.

The excellent teacher/counselor is also able to nudge the client forward, making the learning process enjoyable and encouraging, the teaching clear, and the process predictable. The client learns how to be a *good client* while the teacher is a *good teacher*.

EMBRACING SMALL, 2-DEGREE CHANGES

Imagine making a turn in your car. This involves a series of small steps, from preparing for the turn by using your turn signal, to tapping the brake and then gently accelerating as you turn the corner. Any sudden jolts make the turn uncomfortable and possibly dangerous.

Good marriage counseling is also a series of small moves, joined together to make a larger change. Any change done well is typically done in small, two-degree moves. Change rarely happens in grand gestures, but rather in small increments.

In counseling, it is important to acknowledge these small, two-degree changes. The client may hardly notice them because they are too close to the change process, but the good counselor notices the changes and highlights them. The counselor knows that encouragement is needed to face the next challenge.

Just as the good counselor walks the tightrope between support and confrontation, encouragement and challenge, the client of good counseling walks the tightrope of enjoying and embracing small, incremental, two-degree changes and not being satisfied to stop there.

Good teaching and good counseling share similarities here as well: both reward one small step of growth built upon a previous step of growth, while always pressing forward. Both client and counselor monitor the progress, acknowledging small, incremental steps of progress *and* also pressing for more growth.

This can be an incredibly difficult balance to achieve—supporting and challenging. I've known clients who are so hard on themselves, they couldn't enjoy the fruits of their hard work. I've known others, at the other extreme, who quit counseling after having made the slightest changes, thinking their work was done. Both are likely to be dissatisfied.

Good counseling, like any good learning process, involves the client accepting the pat on the back for hard work done but not stopping after mediocre progress. This is best done by embracing incremental, two-degree steps of progress, which add up to even greater gains over time.

WORK BETWEEN SESSIONS

There is a huge misunderstanding about counseling. Many clients believe counseling only occurs during the session. For real growth to occur, this cannot be true.

For there to be incremental gains over time, relational work must be done in between counseling sessions. It's not always easy to convince clients of the importance of continuity in this work, but good counseling always involves relational work between sessions.

> **FOR REAL GROWTH TO OCCUR WHEN WORKING TO SAVE A MARRIAGE, THE COUPLE MUST DO SOME RELATIONAL WORK BETWEEN COUNSELING SESSIONS.**

Counseling takes up very few hours every week. With 168 hours in the week, there's plenty of time left for practicing what is learned in the counseling—or regressing. Good counseling bridges the gap between sessions by creating continuity between them.

What does continuity of counseling look like? Good counseling encourages clients to read suggested materials, practice the communication tools taught, journal, or simply debrief the insights gained from that week's counseling session. Good counseling links previous sessions to the current one, building new skills upon previously learned ones.

Can you see how key this is for good counseling? The couple who reads the books, practices the exercises, and actually utilizes the tools taught and practiced in counseling stands a far better chance of progressing than the couple who views the counseling session itself as the work. Both counselor and client must make strong efforts to bridge the time between sessions.

CELEBRATING PROGRESS/GOLD STARS

Couples must celebrate their progress. Even if there is little to applaud, they must find those gold-star moments of progress that are highlighted by good counseling.

Counseling is very difficult at times. The hard work done by the client must be recognized and encouraged, fostering a sense of hope that they can learn even more. Good counseling takes note of the moments of progress, knowing that doing so not only instills hope but also serves to keep issues in perspective. A temporary lapse in progress is not necessarily a permanent one.

I worked with a couple recently who were having a particularly difficult time in their marriage. They had experienced ups and downs previously, and this was clearly one of those down times.

Feeling discouraged, they lost sight of the progress they'd made. Discouraged, they focused only on their current struggle. My counseling involved reminding them that they were experiencing a challenging issue, but had overcome similar issues in the past. I reminded them to keep that in mind, to gain perspective.

Additionally, I reminded them that beneath the conflict, they still love each other and are committed to making their marriage work. I encouraged them to remember the hard work they are currently doing, to remember they've had tough times before and made it through them. I reminded them of the really good work they'd done with me in the past and the obstacles they've overcome. Remembering all of these things in down times encourages couples to keep moving forward.

Good counseling involves encouraging couples to step back and remember why they are in this struggle—because they want to stay together, they want to overcome the struggle. The struggle is worth it since they can emerge from it stronger, but they *must* celebrate their progress.

KEEP CHOOSING THE RELATIONSHIP

Brianne and Kent had an initial bad experience in counseling. They pulled back, discouraged and disappointed. They continued to struggle in their marriage. Then they decided to try counseling again, and this time promises to be much more rewarding.

Good marital counseling is helping a couple try again. They don't have to keep trying, of course, if they are really ready to end their relationship. Often, however, couples need encouragement to maintain their determination to save their relationship.

GOOD COUNSELING IS FOR COUPLES WHO CHOOSE TO RENEW THEIR MARRIAGE AGAIN, THIS TIME ON MORE SOLID FOOTING, WITH GREATER SKILLS AND UNDERSTANDING THAT A GOOD MARRIAGE TAKES WORK.

Marriages are renewable relationships. Good counseling is for couples who choose to renew their marriage again, this time on more solid footing, with greater skills and understanding that they can never coast. They must choose their mate, again and again, and the counselor is privileged to be part of that process.

SAYING GOODBYE

Good counseling has a start and a finish. There comes a time, when the counseling has been done well, by both client and counselor, and it's time to say goodbye. This can be a difficult process for both parties. An attachment and connection have been made, an alliance forged. Now, that relationship changes.

The client may drag their feet at ending the counseling; counselors, too, have been known to resist saying goodbye to a couple they have cared so much about. It is another challenging time for both. Yet, both the couple and counselor know, if the counseling has gone well, that it's time for an ending.

This is also a time to reflect on the good work that has been done, a time for both client and counselor to take satisfaction in having done their part to create this good counseling relationship. They can be pleased about the quality and depth of work and the courage it has taken to continue the counseling process through challenging moments.

Whether it is goodbye for now, or goodbye forever, there is often compassion and warmth for both the counselor and client at the prospect of ending their hard, hard work.

CLOSING THOUGHTS

Good marriage counseling may be hard to find, but it can be obtained. It can be found by clients like Brianne and Kent, who were tenacious in seeking out a counselor who met their expectations. It can be attained by others who do their research, learn about good counseling, and settle for nothing less.

Good marriage counseling occurs if both client and counselor seek to uncover expectations, make the unspoken spoken, and are bold enough to talk about what needs to change to create a powerful partnership.

Marriage counseling can be a powerful, life-changing, relationship-changing experience if both client and counselor put energy and effort into the process. The qualities that make for effective counseling are no secret. Knowing how to create a powerful counseling experience, both client and counselor can work to make this process one that is rewarding.

What should be done if you're in counseling that is not working? We'll tackle that issue in our next chapter.

PRELUDE:
TINA AND STAN

"**I** am encouraged," Tina told her husband Stan as they sat in their living room. "I have to admit I never thought we could get back to this place. It feels like we're in a new relationship, or at least the beginning of one."

"I agree," Stan said, smiling. "It's all because of you. I gave up long ago, but you kept fighting for us. You pushed for us to find a counselor we both felt good about. It was an uphill battle, but you kept at it and here we are."

"Firing the other counselor was a hard thing to do," Tina said. "I liked her enough, but she never challenged us. She just listened. I feel like we know so much more about what good counseling looks like now."

"I probably would have kept going to her," Stan admitted quietly. "I didn't see as clearly as you that she required so little of us. That she didn't challenge us. I didn't know what to expect from counseling and figured what we were getting was what it was all about."

"Can you see the difference now, though?" Tina asked. "Can you see how this counselor is night and day different?"

"Oh yeah," Stan said. "I haven't always liked it though. I liked the first counselor. She was nice and sweet, soft and encouraging. This guy is kind of tough. He's a bit confrontational at times, and it keeps me off guard."

"Yes, but he sees our bad patterns and isn't afraid to bring them to our attention," Tina said. "We need someone who's going to look beneath the surface. We need someone who's not afraid to ruffle our feathers. He is sure not going to sit there nodding his head when he sees real trouble."

"He is quick to point out our issues, that's for sure," Stan said. "But even if it is at times uncomfortable, I like that he is not choosing sides, he's not trying to please either one of us. I'm not always comfortable with that, but I think it's helping."

"I am getting more comfortable with being a little uncomfortable," Tina said. "I like that he confronts destructive patterns in both of us. He doesn't let anything slide by."

"I'm just saying it would have been easier with the last counselor," Stan replied. "Maybe not helpful, but it was a whole lot easier to have her just nod and smile."

"And we wouldn't have made the progress we're making now," Tina said. "Would you really prefer the woman we were seeing?"

"Not really," Stan said. "I'm just saying talking to someone who doesn't push is just a simple hour out of my life. Show up and chat. I didn't have to do any work."

"Exactly, and nothing changed," Tina said. "We ended up where we started, and if you recall, I had one foot out the door and the other one close behind. I need someone who will push us to change, who challenges our thinking and old ways of being that are killing us. I know we both have things that *have* to change. We really do."

"You're right," Stan said. "I forget how bad things really were. I guess if we hadn't changed counselors, I'd be the same as before, still acting out, still destructive. And worse, you would have been gone. Thanks for the reminder."

"That last counselor was more uncomfortable pushing us than we were being pushed."

"Yeah," Stan said. "I can see that. The guy we're seeing now is much more confident. He sure doesn't mind confronting bad behaviors in either of us. He knows what he's talking about."

"Confrontation's tough and he's fair. He is not letting either of us get away with our bad habits," Tina said.

Tina stopped and looked over at Stan.

"I guess that's really the difference between someone who does a little bit of counseling and someone who specializes in marriage counseling. This guy knows what it takes to really bring about change."

Tina paused again.

"This is going to take hard work for both of us. I'm just glad we found someone who knows what we need to do to change our bad patterns. We need to let this counselor do what he's trained to do."

"I know I don't always see things as clearly or quickly as you do," Stan said. "You see what needs to change faster than I do."

"Maybe so," Tina said. "But I need you to be present at our sessions, and I need to know you will ask questions to help you understand how change for us can happen, to be tuned into our marriage and what is and isn't working. I'd like for you to notice if I'm happy or not."

"I think I'm beginning to get it," Stan said. "It's not too late, is it? I'm starting to understand what the counselor is saying. I'm understanding his points quicker now and I'm getting it. I agree with him. I feel happy about the changes I think I'm making and want to keep up the counseling with him until we both feel like we're ready to do this on our own."

"Thank you," Tina said. "I'd love you to lead the way. I'd love to know you're watching out for me and for our marriage."

"I am, Tina," Stan said. "Trust me. I'm learning more all the time."

"Great," Tina said. "I feel lucky to be where we're at. We can move beyond crisis mode and begin growing again with the skills we're learning."

"Here's to our renewed marriage," Stan said.

MAKING COUNSELING WORK FOR YOU

Being confident of this, that he who began a good work in you will carry it on to completion.
—Philippians 1:6

We have covered a lot of ground. We've discussed the challenges of marriage. We've discussed the desperation that couples in troubled marriages feel and how their distress is amplified by their difficulty when searching to find real help.

It is a horrible situation for couples who try everything they know to do, only to have it end with an ineffective counselor.

Couples have a right to be indignant about counselors who let them down. We've talked about the qualities of bad counselors and what to watch out for. We've also talked about the qualities of good counselors and good counseling.

You've done your work and found a counselor you think will work with you and for you. You've searched for and found a counselor you think can help you turn your marriage around. All you have to do now is show up, and things are going to get better, right?

Probably not. What about what *you* bring to the counseling sessions?

It's time to turn to your role in making counseling work. It does no good to lament efforts made in the past that didn't work out. It's time to work with your spouse and your counselor to create a counseling process that turns bad habits into good ones, destructive patterns into healthy ones.

By combining all of the information from the previous chapters and applying it in your counseling, you can create the most powerful, life-changing process possible. It's time now for you to take this information, this new learning about the difference between a bad client and a good one, and be the best client possible.

Seasoned counselors know there is such a thing as a bad client. They also know when they're working with a couple who desperately wants to change and will stop at nothing to make counseling work for them. These counselors know the difference between a couple who will likely sabotage their counseling process and quit prematurely and a couple who enhances the likelihood of counseling going well. They recognize the couple who will dig in and work on themselves and their marriage and those who will quit practically as soon as they've started.

So, let's bring our work to a focus. Let's take all the information from previous chapters and all we learn in this chapter and lean into being a good client working with a good counselor, making the most of counseling.

BEING A GOOD CLIENT

The first requirement for being a good client is understanding and taking responsibility for being one. Your counselor can only do so much. In the end, you are responsible for discerning the difference between a *bad client* and a *good client*. Learning the difference is in your control.

Furthermore, *you* are responsible for *being* a good client. *You* are the one able to have a huge impact on whether marriage counseling goes well or goes poorly.

Perhaps you're thinking, *But Dr. Hawkins, you've spent numerous chapters talking about the qualities of bad counselors.*

It's true—and there *are* bad counselors. But by grasping the concept of being a good client, and the responsibility that goes along with it, *you* influence the counselor and counseling.

Going to counseling is a big step, but it's only the first step. There are many additional steps you must take after putting aside the doubts you have about counseling and any tendency to be passive in this process. Much of the success of counseling rests on you being the best client possible—and I'll tell you how to do that.

Take a moment and reflect on the fact that you have already read most of this book and are considering counseling. Let's build upon that huge step. You're armed with a lot of information about counseling. Now, take the next step forward and embrace the different skills needed to make counseling work for you.

SHOWING UP

A lot of people go to one or two counseling sessions and then drop out. This lack of commitment and passivity baffles counselors. Why would anyone go to the expense and effort of finding a counselor only to drop out after a few sessions? Yet that is exactly what happens.

> **YOU CANNOT POSSIBLY MAKE PROGRESS ON YOUR GOALS IF YOU DON'T DEDICATE YOURSELF TO SHOWING UP FOR COUNSELING.**

Your first task in becoming a good counselee is to make the commitment to show up, again and again, when you feel encouraged and when you feel discouraged. You cannot possibly make progress on your goals if you don't dedicate yourself, first and foremost, to showing up.

Your first task in becoming a good counselee is to make the commitment to show up, again and again, when you feel encouraged and when you feel discouraged. You cannot possibly make progress on your goals if you don't dedicate yourself, first and foremost, to showing up.

Showing up conveys a powerful truth to the counselor that you are committed to both the counseling and to growth. It says you are wholeheartedly invested in this counseling process. It says you are going to put all of your effort into the counseling, and you expect them to do the same.

Let me assure you of something: when I sense a client is fully invested and fully involved, it impacts me. I know, as a counselor, I must be as involved as they are. If they bring passion, commitment, and focus to the session, I'm likely to bring the same. If they show up intermittently, this conveys a lack of sincerity and heart.

Showing up is key.

Just this week, I considered (again) cancelling my piano lesson. I told myself that I was too busy to keep it. I had a lot of things on my calendar and considered canceling a legitimate choice.

My wife nudged me forward.

"You know you're just making an excuse," she said. "You'll regret it if you cancel. You're not going to make the progress you want to make."

"But I'm too busy," I replied.

"You've always got something going on," she said. "How important is it for you to keep up your lessons?"

"You're right," I said. "It is important."

I kept the lesson.

I shared my near-cancellation with my piano teacher, Claire. She pointed out that it's important to keep the routine of lessons; otherwise, one excuse builds upon another and before you know it, you'll be out of the routine.

Even more, whether it was my best lesson or not, *she* appreciated my efforts. I impacted her with my commitment.

We all know this to be true. Whether we're talking about exercising, sticking to a healthy diet, attending church, taking Spanish or piano lessons, or engaging in counseling, we've got to show up. We need to make firm, clear decisions about our intentions, goals, and desired outcomes.

If your counseling is beneficial and helping you toward your goals, show up and remind yourself *why* you are showing up.

KNOWING YOUR COUNSELING GOALS

Along with your decision to show up for counseling, be clear about why you are in counseling and what you hope to get from it. This is critical knowledge for you. While your counselor can certainly help you refine your goals, you must show up with an idea of what you want to accomplish.

Are you hoping to find solutions to ongoing problems plaguing your marriage? Perhaps you want to discover the destructive patterns that send your marriage spiraling downward and what you're contributing to this destructive process.

I'm not suggesting you need to arrive at your first counseling session with a list of goals, but you must have some idea about what feels wrong and what you want changed. This should be your first order of business. Why have you come to counseling and what must change? Don't be too concerned if you're still a bit confused about your goals. Your counselor will help you clarify them and help you develop a counseling plan.

Most who attend couples counseling for the first time are confused about what will happen. This is understandable. It takes time to settle into, and learn about, being a good client. When you finally go, set your sights high. Go with anticipation and expectation. Expect more rather than less from counseling. Don't lower your sights—raise them. You're meeting with a specialist, and partnering with them should bring about change. It's a time to learn new relationship skills and dust off old skills. It's a time to improve communication skills, learn patience and forgiveness, and cultivate empathy, trust, and honesty. It's also a time to learn about selflessness, caring, and giving to another.

Remember, tap into your motivation for counseling and remind your-self about it often. You want change. You need change. Insist that your counselor help you in this process.

COUNSELING IS COLLABORATIVE

Entering into counseling may be one of the most significant decisions you ever make. You're entering a collaborative relationship and making counseling work means you must be frank, direct, and vulnerable.

Your counselor cannot read your mind. You must tell them what you're thinking and what you expect from counseling. Tell them your hopes and fears. After you've shared, ask if they are able to help you. Will they partner with you to reach your goals?

Pay close attention to their response. Are they emphatic when they say they can help? Are they eager to partner with you in this most vital, collaborative process?

Counseling involves teamwork. Self-protection will not serve you well here. You must allow this professional to know your innermost thoughts and feelings. This can be frightening, but the decision not to hide, not to cover up, is a powerful decision. Vulnerability can be a real strength.

COUNSELING CANNOT WORK IF YOU ARE GUARDED OR PASSIVE. YOU MUST OPEN UP AND SPEAK ABOUT WHAT YOU'RE THINKING AND FEELING.

Counseling can only work if the client and counselor both fulfill their responsibility. As the client, your job is to bring openness, direct-ness, and vulnerability. The counseling cannot work if you are guarded or passive. While it is human nature to be self-protective, counseling relies on candor. You must open up and speak about what you're thinking and feeling. Counseling only works when you are fully open and emotionally engaged.

You should remind yourself of this engagement repeatedly. Any temptation to hold back will thwart efforts by the counselor in getting to know you. They must get to know your innermost thoughts and feelings if they are to be helpful.

You and the counselor are a team, working together on a common goal. Your counselor wants you to succeed in reaching your goals. If they say or do anything that hampers the relationship, *talk about it immediately*. Help your counselor help you by reminding yourself of this partnership.

BEING READY TO CHANGE

Your situation is undoubtedly thorny, perhaps even urgent. Because of that, it is important that you show up ready to work. You must show up with the assumption that you are doing some things wrong and need to make a change.

This can be a difficult truth to accept because most of us assume we are right. Clinging to our beliefs, we rehearse how what we think is correct.

This attitude will ruin any chance of success in counseling. Why? Because counseling means being open to change. It means going to counseling with the belief that you are likely doing many things that harm your marriage and need a specialist to speak into those destructive beliefs and actions.

I typically inform those counseling with me that I'm a *change agent*— my job is to challenge how you view matters and confront self-destructive patterns of behavior. As you might imagine, this is not always received warmly.

Most of us are double-minded. We want to change and we simultaneously want to stay the same. We want to magically feel better without having to give up well-worn attitudes and behaviors. While we want to feel better, we resist change.

Since I'm a change agent, and my clients want to change, they must be open and ready to change. I take this so seriously that I ask each new couple coming to see me two very important questions:

1. Do I have permission to speak into your lives? (They *always* say "yes.")

2. Do you give each other permission to speak into each other's lives? (They *always* hesitate but ultimately grant permission.)

I'm not surprised by either answer. The first question and answer are obvious. The couple has come seeking my expertise. It would be ridiculous if they told me they wanted to talk but didn't really want any counseling, advice, or observations. Change would be impossible.

Perhaps not surprisingly, I often remind couples of their desire for change and point out that for change to occur, I am required to speak into their lives. I must remind them that they gave me permission to challenge their thinking and actions.

The second answer never surprises me either. Because many couples arrive at counseling with a history of distrust for each other, they often resist giving permission to their mate to offer feedback. However, I share that for couples counseling to be effective, they must be able to share observations without defensiveness. This often takes work, but good counseling is able to create an openness and receptivity to feedback.

I remind couples that as painful as it might be, they must get to the point where they value feedback. Emotional and relational growth demands hearing what your mate has to say and applying it to your life. There is no shortcut around this.

WORKING BETWEEN COUNSELING SESSIONS

I've already noted that there are 168 hours in a week and only a small number of those hours will be in counseling. This creates a real problem. The counseling partnership is a collaborative process. The team—the couple and the counselor—seeks substantial change. This is challenging when the partners spend only one or two hours a week together in counseling.

What is the answer?

This doesn't mean you coast for the remaining hours of the week. No. For counseling to be robust and powerful, you must participate in homework assignments, practice communication and conflict-resolution skills, read materials assigned to you, and make journal entries regarding issues that arise between sessions.

Homework assignments will vary with each individual couple. One couple might find reading the Bible's Song of Songs together rekindles their romantic feelings for one another. Another couple might need to give each other space to pursue hobbies. Trading chores for a week or preparing dinner together are other options. Every couple is different—and it's up to the couple and the counselor to figure out what will help to restore their marriage.

Making counseling work means thinking about your counseling session, making use of the insights from it, and planning ahead for the next session. In this way, you link sessions together into a cohesive whole. You create bridges between sessions so they actually flow together. Your counseling becomes more cohesive, connected, and dynamic.

Remember, the ultimate goal of counseling is to help you learn and gain expertise in relationship skills so that there will come a time when you no longer need counseling.

FOCUS ON PROCESS GOALS

Making counseling work means having specific goals, but perhaps not always in the way you think.

Dr. Patrick Keelan, a psychologist in Calgary, Alberta, Canada, notes the importance of focusing on process goals. He explains:

Athletes and other performers do their best by focusing on process goals. Process goals are actions you can perform which are within your control and which are most likely to lead to a top performance. Performers who focus on results—also known as outcome goals—don't tend to perform as well because the focus on results detracts from their doing what they need to do to get the job done. Just as in sports, focusing on process goals in counselling leads to the best progress…by learning and applying the skills which are the process goals your therapist recommends you work on to make progress. Clients who don't focus on "doing the work" and become preoccupied with discussions of their progress make less progress.[17]

This is a powerful concept. For me, focusing on process goals means paying attention to the skills I'm learning, like my piano and tennis lessons, not on whether I'm actually getting better. In counseling, it means focusing on specific skills and not worrying about whether you've arrived at your goal.

FOCUS ON ACTIONS WITHIN YOUR CONTROL

Closely related to the power and importance of process goals is learning to focus on what is within your control. Focusing on something we cannot directly change creates frustration and discouragement. Focusing on your mate's behavior and being unable to directly impact it is disheartening.

However, focusing on what is in your control, your own thoughts and behavior, is encouraging. This involves *staying on your side of the street*. It's about changing yourself rather than focusing on what you think your mate needs to change.

It has been said that every ounce of energy you use to manipulate or control another person is energy you no longer have to change yourself. It's wasted energy.

This is a very difficult truth to master. It is tempting and natural to focus on your mate because of your feelings of hurt and anger. Because you are so unhappy, you may even choose to talk about them exclusively in counseling. This is a mistake—and it's something you have the power to change.

Please understand that your mate's behavior is relevant, but only insofar as what you have the power to do about it. It is natural to feel irritated, hurt, and frustrated with them. However, your focus must always be on

17. Dr. Patrick Keelan, "Ten Ways to Get the Most Out of Counselling" (drpatrickkeelan. com/psychology/ten-ways-to-get-the-most-out-of-counselling).

what *you* can do about the problem. While it's important to note what it is that your mate is doing that troubles you, and your feelings about it, this reflection must lead to effective problem-solving. Focus on what *you* can do to change the relationship. Determine what you want to do regarding the issues within your mate that bother you.

> **WHILE YOUR MATE MAY DO OR SAY SOMETHING YOU DON'T LIKE, YOU CAN ONLY CHANGE YOUR OWN THOUGHTS, FEELINGS, AND ACTIONS, NOT THEIRS.**

Returning your focus on *you* is empowering. You are the one you control. You control your thoughts, feelings, and actions, and these can lead you to making powerful changes. Think about it. Complaining about your mate may feel satisfying in the moment, but eventually, you will feel discouraged because you cannot directly impact change. Focusing on ways you *can* impact change is enlivening.

Focus on you and what actions you can take.

PROBLEM-SOLVE RATHER THAN RUMINATE

Focusing on your mate leads to rumination and even greater discouragement. Making counseling work means catching yourself complaining and brooding and shifting to problem-solving. Teamwork with your counselor can help you with this problem.

Most of us get caught on the proverbial hamster wheel of fussing and fuming about what others have done to us rather than spending a little time thinking constructively about what actions we need to take about those problems.

Those who make counseling work for them are focused on the skills needed to change their life and relationship circumstances.

Radical acceptance is a powerful concept that can help us get unstuck and take responsibility for our lives. Radical acceptance means we accept that we didn't get where we are today by one misstep. Rather, we have made a long series of choices that have established patterns leading to our unhappiness.

Subsequently, this means for change to occur, we must not play the victim and rant about what others are doing to us. Rather, we must accept that we have allowed troubling patterns of behavior by others and ourselves to develop over a long period of time. Accepting our part in these problems is a powerful step toward not simply venting or complaining but taking effective action instead.

Our circumstances will change when we change. Making counseling work for you means ending the complaints and shifting to powerful action.

PATIENCE IN COUNSELING

Pace is critical in making counseling work for you. It means cultivating patience toward the counseling process. We're often so close to our lives, our thoughts, and our feelings that we can't see the progress we're making. Being one step back, your counselor can see the headway that you've made.

Additionally, counseling is not about making steady progress. It often means taking two steps forward and one step back. Sometimes there are simply bad days when it seems nothing is working.

Yet, if you show up, commit to the process, and remain open and teachable, progress will occur. In fact, this is where good counseling comes in. Your counselor helps you keep things in perspective. A bad day, when you lapse into old behavior, doesn't mean you're not making progress. Your counselor will remind you of the overall progress you're making and help you accept the relapse as part of the process.

So, easy does it. Changing longstanding patterns is hard work. If you want to make changes that will stick, you need to have a long-term perspective. You need to be kind to yourself and your mate and repeatedly acknowledge your progress.

USING BOTH INDIVIDUAL AND COUPLES COUNSELING

Not all issues in a marriage can be attributed equally to both spouses. It takes a partnership with your counselor to determine whose issue is whose. A marriage is a partnership of two distinct, fallible human beings. Sometimes, one of you needs time to really investigate your life apart from your mate.

Often, marital counseling involves some combination of individual and couples counseling because some problems are directly related to the relationship, and some are issues of an individual.

Take, for example, a spouse who has issues with anger. A husband may say, "My wife makes me angry," but this is technically not true, since we all have choices in how we respond to situations. While there may be legitimate issues in the relationship that play a role in provoking anger, this may require individual attention.

It's imperative to be open to the difference between individual issues and those pertaining to the couple. When your focus is on you and what you can do to improve yourself and your marriage, you'll be open to the possibility of individual counseling. You may, in fact, prefer it at times. Stepping back and focusing on yourself can be a respite from the tangled interactions you may experience with your mate.

How can you know if there is individual work to be done? Here are a few questions to ask:

+ Are you often unable to manage your emotional response when problem-solving with your mate?

+ Do your current marriage issues remind you of earlier struggles in your childhood home or environment?

+ Do you find it challenging to step back from your marriage issues to be able to enjoy the rest of your life?

If you answered "yes" to any of these questions, individual counseling may be of great benefit to you. Again, your counselor will be able to help you make this decision.

TRUSTING YOUR COUNSELOR

Your collaborative relationship with your counselor requires huge amounts of trust, which may be difficult for many reasons. You will put a great deal of work into your marriage counseling, so it is requisite for your trust in your counselor to remain strong.

One of the key aspects of trust is a willingness to be vulnerable. Can you trust that your counselor has your best interests in mind when they ask you to share your inner thoughts and tender feelings? Do you trust they will help you feel safe and cared for even as they confront aspects of your character that disrupt your marriage?

Gaining as much as you can from counseling means trusting your counselor is able to see what you cannot see because they have knowledge you do not have and can ascertain what skills you need.

Trust is, of course, not an all-or-nothing concept. You can learn to trust your counselor gradually over time. You can share when you need a little more tender loving care than normal. You can ask that they treat certain subjects with greater sensitivity.

Ultimately, however, if you're going to make counseling work for you, you'll strongly consider your counselor's advice and apply it to your own reasoning of the situation.

PREPARE FOR YOUR NEXT SESSION

Good counseling is a collaborative partnership that involves making sense of your life. You must prepare for your counseling sessions to benefit from them.

One of the primary reasons anyone seeks counseling is to gain clarity, to create an understanding of their life. This means you must pay close attention to what troubles you and what you talk about in counseling. Your counseling, as we've already said, must be connected so the issues become clearer over time.

You might ask, "Why am I so unhappy?" or, "What am I doing wrong?" or perhaps, "Why am I being treated the way I am?"

These common questions are efforts to make sense of what is happening, to develop a cohesive story about your life so you know what needs to change and what might remain the same. By talking out various problems, you begin to see patterns. Life begins to make sense. You begin to see ways of interacting that cause strife, again and again.

This can only happen with preparation.

Making counseling work for you means doing your part to reflect on what you're learning in counseling. You and your counselor will weave a cohesive story out of your life. You learn to make the pieces of your life fit together like a complex jigsaw puzzle. After enough pieces are in place, it starts to make sense. Through journaling, reflection, prayer, and counseling, you come to see the same problems repeat. You see the patterns and begin to see your part in those problems. This leads naturally to knowing what must change.

Now, becoming more watchful and insightful, you bring your observations to your counseling session; together with your counselor, you fit even more pieces of your life puzzle together. Your life begins to make sense and now you have more choices for change.

IF YOU WANT TO MAKE COUNSELING WORK, YOU MUST NOTICE WHAT IS HAPPENING IN YOUR LIFE, DISCOVER THE PATTERNS, AND SHARE THE CLUES THAT EMERGE WITH YOUR COUNSELOR.

There is no room for being a passive participant. This is your life and no one, not even your counselor, will take your life as seriously as you do. If you want to really make counseling work, it is your job to notice what is happening in your life from week to week and discover the patterns. Emotional laziness won't serve you well. You must take an active interest in your life, see the clues emerging, and share them with your counselor. Your counselor will listen to your insights and help you develop a plan for change going forward.

LEARNING TO TOLERATE SHORT-TERM DISCOMFORT

Good counseling can be exciting, but it can also be uncomfortable. It's never enjoyable to be told we play a role in our marital problems or have our shortcomings aired in counseling, especially in front of our spouse. This takes strength of character and, of course, humility.

But pride has no place in our change process, so we must share and listen to what our counselor has to say. Giving our counselor's insights a chance to sink in and trying out new behaviors means experiencing discomfort. Counseling is about both feeling relief and feeling discomfort. We must expect that.

Counseling is about change, which means disrupting the status quo. It's about disrupting old patterns of thinking and behaving, being challenged to think in new ways. A good counselor points out where our old ways of coping are actually causing us more harm than good, and a good client incorporates this feedback into their life.

Like it or not, it's important to experience short-term anxiety in the counseling process. It is in facing anxiety-producing situations that we give ourselves a chance to grow. We learn that whatever is triggering our anxiety is not as dangerous as we imagined, and we can determine to grow beyond it.

I have discovered though my own marriage I can be a *pouter*. This is a long-term pattern I developed at an early age, a coping method that served me well when I was afraid of sharing my feelings with my parents.

This pattern of coping no longer works. In fact, it is infuriating to my wife—and rightly so. Having insight about this problem has been helpful, but insight doesn't always bring change. I've had to be confronted with this pattern and gone through numerous times of discomfort while trying to change it.

Change, by necessity, involves discomfort, and anyone in counseling knows this.

TRYING OUT NEW BEHAVIORS

It's one thing to be told our behavior must change if we want the positive results; it's another matter to go through the process of change.

Not only is counseling a place where we learn what needs to change, it's also where we can practice changing. We leave the counseling office with instructions about what to change and how to change it, then go through the week trying on new behaviors. This can be a painful and challenging process.

This change process can also be exciting.

Recently, I studied how change occurs neurologically. While I'm not prepared to explain it in depth, my understanding is that we can literally change our minds if we *intend* to change our minds. I tried this out a year ago at Thanksgiving.

My wife Christie announced to me that we would be having more guests over for Thanksgiving than originally planned. I cringed when I considered the number of people we would be hosting in our small cottage. My old behavior of being *put out* when facing an emotionally challenging situation confronted my new resolve to be more social and engaging.

Faced with my *old self* and my *new ideal self*, I determined to be warm, agreeable, and inviting toward everyone coming to our home for the holiday. I planned how I wanted to act differently; more precisely, I imagined myself being loving and engaging. I rehearsed enjoying myself and appreciating everyone who came.

When the day arrived, I thought and acted differently. I tried out my new behavior, and the results were quite remarkable. I enjoyed the guests and later heard they enjoyed being in our home for this festive occasion.

Making counseling work is about envisioning who you want to be, individually and in relationship. It's about rehearsing new behavior after you've identified what old behaviors need to be changed. It's about identifying old thoughts, attitudes, and behaviors, and then changing them, one step at a time.

WHEN TO FIRE YOUR COUNSELOR

Making your counseling work means being vigilant about it and watching it vigorously for any indication it might not be working.

> **IF YOU ARE DISSATISFIED WITH COUNSELING AT ANY TIME, BRINGING YOUR CONCERNS TO THE ATTENTION OF THE COUNSELOR GIVES THEM A CHANCE TO MAKE ADJUSTMENTS.**

If you are dissatisfied at any time, you must bring your concerns to the attention of your counselor. They will not necessarily sense when you are satisfied or dissatisfied with the counseling. Bringing your concerns to the attention of the counselor gives them a chance to make adjustments. They will help you discuss what might be getting in the way of better counseling and will help you make your decision, even if it means no longer working with them.

You now know the qualities of a good counselor, so you have a great starting point from which to decide if you're working with the right person. In addition to the qualities we've listed throughout this book, it may also come down to a pure *gut reaction*. If it feels like counseling is adding stress to your life rather than relieving it, if you find yourself dreading counseling and don't particularly like your counselor, it may be time to say goodbye to them.

Terminating counseling is rarely easy. Your counselor may resist your decision. If you are sure and clear, be direct and firm. Tell your counselor why you are ending the counseling and then end the relationship. Your decision never needs to be irreversible; you can let your counselor know you'll return if the decision feels right.

Trust your instincts. Listen to your gut and go with it.

SEE CHALLENGES AS OPPORTUNITIES

Overcoming challenges leads to self-confidence and emotional growth. This is true when it comes to learning a new language, acquiring a new skill, or overcoming an obstacle.

Counseling is largely about facing challenges and experiencing growth when that occurs. Counseling is about the process of growth and learning to embrace growth as having value in and of itself. In other words, counseling is not only about achieving goals, as important as that is, but also about embracing challenges as opportunities for change.

Every time your feathers are ruffled—every time you are annoyed, frightened, or discouraged—you have an opportunity to look inward to see what's going on. Identifying these areas of weakness is the starting point for real change.

Again, your faith will help you. Scripture says we are bound to face adversity in our lives. What we do with that adversity is key. *"Consider it pure joy, my brothers and sisters, whenever you face trials of many kinds, because you know the testing of your faith produces perseverance"* (James 1:2–3).

Challenges are an opportunity to grow our faith. These same challenges are also an opportunity to press into our counseling experience and ask some questions of ourselves and our counselor.

The experienced client learns to get excited about facing and overcoming challenges and problems. Yes, you heard me right. Challenges and relationship problems shine a light on something not working and open the door to emotional growth. This leads to improved relationships.

CLOSING THOUGHTS

We have arrived at the end of this book. We have journeyed a long way together, learning about why marriages fail and why marriage counseling typically fails.

You have learned about what constitutes a bad counselor and what differentiates them from a good counselor. You've learned how to choose a counselor who will be able to walk with you and guide you.

Most importantly, you've learned how to make counseling a positive experience for you and your partner, and the critical part you play by being a good client. You've discovered ways you can make your counseling more powerful and learned it is okay to terminate counseling if you believe it is not helping.

In closing, remember that counseling is ultimately your responsibility. It is your task to search for a counselor who fits you and then to work hard to make the changes needs to bring health to your marriage. You will know it's the right fit because you will learn to embrace growth, seek change, and tolerate discomfort on the path to healing. You must be honest, open, and willing, and if you do your part, chances are good your mate and the counselor will do their part.

Are you ready for your next counseling session? It's time to apply all you've learned and practice, practice, practice.

ABOUT THE AUTHOR

Dr. David Hawkins, MBA, MSW, MA, PhD, is a clinical psychologist who has brought healing and restoration to thousands of marriages and individuals since he began his work in 1976. He is passionate about helping couples heal marriage wounds and rediscover deeper connection and intimacy.

In addition to marriage counseling, Dr. Hawkins is a leader in the field of treatment for narcissism and emotional abuse in the context of relationships.

Dr. Hawkins is the founder of the Marriage Recovery Center. A speaker and trainer for the American Association of Christian Counselors, he writes for Crosswalk.com, CBN.org, and Believe.com, and has made regular appearances on Moody Radio and Faith Radio. Dr. Hawkins is a best-selling author of over thirty books, including *When Pleasing Others Is Hurting You*, *When Loving Him Is Hurting You*, and *Dealing with the CrazyMakers in Your Life*.

He earned his doctorate and master's degree in psychology from George Fox University. He also received his MBA from Strayer University and a master's in social work from Portland State University.

Dr. Hawkins and his wife Christie live on Bainbridge Island in Washington State.

Welcome to Our House!

We Have a Special Gift for You

It is our privilege and pleasure to share in your love of Christian books. We are committed to bringing you authors and books that feed, challenge, and enrich your faith.

To show our appreciation, we invite you to sign up to receive a specially selected **Reader Appreciation Gift**, with our compliments. Just go to the Web address at the bottom of this page.

God bless you as you seek a deeper walk with Him!

WE HAVE A GIFT FOR YOU. VISIT:

whpub.me/nonfictionthx

WHITAKER
HOUSE